BAPTISTWAY®

Adult Bible Teaching Guide

Amos, Hosea, Micah

Bruce Cresson
David Roberts
Mike Harton
Melvin and Jane Warren
Craig West

BAPTISTWAY PRESS®
Dallas, Texas

Amos, Hosea, Micah—Adult Bible Teaching Guide

Copyright © 2003 by BAPTISTWAY PRESS®.
All rights reserved.

Printed in the United States of America.

BAPTISTWAY PRESS® Management Team

Executive Director, Baptist General Convention of Texas: Charles Wade
Coordinator, Church Health and Growth Section: H. Lynn Eckeberger
Director, Bible Study/Discipleship Center: Dennis Parrott

Publishing consultant: Ross West, Positive Difference Communications
Cover and Interior Design and Production: Desktop Miracles, Inc.
Front Cover Photo: Samaria, BiblePlaces.com

First edition: June 2003
ISBN: 1–931060–37–1

How to Make the Best Use of This Teaching Guide

Leading a class in studying the Bible is a sacred trust. This *Teaching Guide* has been prepared to help you as you give your best to this important task.

In each lesson, you will find first "Bible Comments" for teachers, to aid you in your study and preparation. The three sections of "Bible Comments" are "Understanding the Context," "Interpreting the Scriptures," and "Focusing on the Meaning." "Understanding the Context" provides a summary overview of the entire background passage that also sets the passage in the context of the Bible book being studied. "Interpreting the Scriptures" provides verse-by-verse comments on the focal passage. "Focusing on the Meaning" offers help with the meaning and application of the focal text.

The second main part of each lesson is "Teaching Plans." You'll find two complete teaching plans in this section. The first is called "Teaching Plan—Varied Learning Activities," and the second is called "Teaching Plan—Lecture and Questions." Choose the plan that best fits your class and your style of teaching. You may also use and adapt ideas from both. Each plan is intended to be practical, helpful, and immediately useful as you prepare to teach. The major headings in each teaching plan are intended to help you sequence how you teach so as to follow the flow of how people tend to learn. The first major heading, "Connect with Life," provides ideas that will help you begin the class session where your class is and draw your class into the study. The second major heading, "Guide Bible Study," offers suggestions for helping your class engage the Scriptures actively and develop a greater understanding of this portion of the Bible's message. The third major heading, "Encourage Application," is meant to help participants focus on how to respond with their lives to this message.

As you and your class begin the study, take time to lead them in writing the date on which each lesson will be studied on the first page of each lesson and/or on the contents page of the *Study Guide*. You may also find it helpful to make and post a chart that indicates the date on which each lesson will be studied. If all of your class has e-mail, send them an e-mail with the dates the lessons will be studied.

Here are some steps you can take to help you prepare well to teach each lesson and save time in doing so:

1. Start early in the week before your class meets.

2. Overview the study in the *Study Guide*. Look at the table of contents, read the study introduction, and read the unit introduction for the lesson you are about to study. Try to see how each lesson relates to the unit and overall study of which it is a part.

3. Consider carefully the suggested Main Idea, Question to Explore, and Teaching Aim. These can help you discover the main thrust of this particular lesson.

4. Use your Bible to read and consider prayerfully the Scripture passages for the lesson. (Each writer of the Bible comments in both the *Teaching Guide* and the *Study Guide* has chosen a favorite translation. You're free to use the Bible translation you prefer and compare it with the translations chosen, of course.)

5. After reading all the Scripture passages in your Bible, then read the Bible comments in the *Study Guide*. The Bible comments are intended to be an aid to your study of the Bible. Read also the small articles—"sidebars"—in each lesson. They are intended to provide additional, enrichment information and inspiration and to encourage thought and application. Try to answer for yourself the questions included in each lesson. They're intended to encourage further thought and application, and you can also use them in the class session itself. Continue your Bible study with the aid of the Bible comments included in this *Teaching Guide*.

6. Review the "Teaching Plans" in this *Teaching Guide*. Consider how these suggestions would help you teach this Bible passage in your class to accomplish the teaching aim.

7. Consider prayerfully the needs of your class and how to teach so you can help your class learn best.

8. Develop and follow a lesson plan based on the suggestions in this *Teaching Guide*, with alterations as needed for your class.

9. Enjoy leading your class in discovering the meaning of the Scripture passages and in applying these passages to their lives.

In addition, you may want to get the enrichment teaching help that is provided in both the printed and internet editions of the *Baptist Standard*. Call 214–630–4571 to begin your subscription to the *Baptist Standard*. Access the internet information by checking the *Baptist Standard* website at http://www.baptiststandard.com. (Other class participants may find this information helpful, too.)

Amos, Hosea, Micah

M I C A H

What the Lord Requires

Focal Text
Amos 2:4–16

Background
Amos 1—2

Main Idea
We, like ancient Israel, must first be concerned about our sins, our acts of injustice, rather than being preoccupied with other's sins and acts of injustice.

Question to Explore
Whose sin does God really want us to focus on?

Teaching Aim
To help the class acknowledge the need to focus on their sins and their part in our society's injustices

A M O S

A God Who Roars

Lesson One

It's for You

BIBLE COMMENTS

Understanding the Context

Amos lived in the middle of the eighth century BC and served as a prophet for God in Israel about 760–750 BC. The nation of the Hebrews had divided into a southern kingdom (called Judah) and a northern kingdom (called Israel or Ephraim) after the death of Solomon in 922 BC (1 Kings 12).

Amos's home was in Tekoa, a small isolated village in Judah, about six miles south of Bethlehem. Tekoa is located at the edge of a desert-like area stretching east from the hill country to the shores of the Dead Sea. There are small fields which can be planted with grains or other plants, but the terrain is clearly suited to grazing sheep and goats.

Although Amos lived in an isolated area, he knew what was happening in the world of his time. He served effectively as a messenger of God, primarily to Israel but also to the surrounding nations. He spoke clearly and boldly, declaring how God responded not only to the events in Israel and Judah, but also God's concerns with the other nations around them. Amos's message was one of divine judgment on the sinful nations.

Amos 1:1 sets the time of his prophetic ministry as in the days of Uzziah, king of Judah (783–742 BC) and Jeroboam, king of Israel (786–746 BC). Jeroboam, son of Joash, is usually called Jeroboam II to distinguish him from Jeroboam son of Nebat, who led the revolt against Solomon's son, Rehoboam in 922 BC. The reference to "two years before the earthquake" does not help in dating Amos, since there is no other known record of this event.

The major power in the Near Eastern world in Amos's day was Assyria, located in the northern part of the valley between the Tigris and Euphrates Rivers. Today this is partly in northern Iraq and partly in southeastern Turkey. Almost a century before the time of Amos, the Assyrian kings had been moving aggressively toward Israel and the neighboring nations. These small nations had allied themselves together and defeated the Assyrian army at a place called Qarqar, on the Orontes River in Syria, in 853 BC. Ahab was the king of Israel at that time. Although this battle is not mentioned in the Bible, Ahab is named as one of its major leaders in an inscription, called the Black Obelisk, left by the Assyrian king, Shalmaneser III.[1] Since that time Assyria had been growing in strength at home but had not been aggressive toward other nations.

In this time of peace and national security for Israel, the nation grew strong. This was the time of the greatest strength of the nation since the days of David and Solomon. But along with this international peace and internal political and military strength, Israel was experiencing serious moral and religious decay.

Jeroboam II led the nation of Israel to a time of growing prosperity. But, as is often the case, while the rich became richer, the poor became poorer. Religious worship was certainly present, even abounding, but it was either insincere or directed to idol gods.

The people in Israel were self-satisfied and felt secure, seeing nothing to threaten their comfortable lifestyle.

Amos was among the shepherds of Tekoa. We do not know whether he had large or small flocks. From illustrations in the messages he proclaimed we can be certain that he knew first-hand the life of a shepherd, and that he was not merely the manager of an extensive sheep ranch. A distinctive Hebrew word is used for shepherds in verse 1. It identifies a particular breed of sheep—small and producing a desirable black wool. We can conclude that he was producing wool rather than sheep for slaughter.

The only other personal information about Amos appears in 7:14, where he tells us three things: he was a herdsman, he was neither a prophet's son nor a professional prophet, and he was a "dresser of sycamore trees." The exact meaning of "dresser of sycamore trees" has been debated, but he was pruning or treating these trees in some way. The sycamore involved was not the sycamore known in America today but was a fruit-producing tree.

A few of these trees can be found today in Amos's home country. The tree produces a small fig-like fruit that lacks the size and desirable flavor of figs. These trees would not survive in the near-desert environment of Tekoa. They would flourish, however, in the more fertile and better watered valleys of the Northern Kingdom of Israel. Amos would have been a regular visitor to Israel in this "moonlighting" occupation of sycamore "dressing." Amos was not an outsider who came north to condemn his neighbor nation; he knew from first-hand observation the religious and moral situation in the nation.

Beyond these facts about Amos, we can gather more from his prophetic sermons—his intelligence, his speaking ability, his clear insight, his knowledge of world affairs, his awareness of the life of the people, and his religious commitment. He certainly was fearless, for he did not hesitate to speak harsh words even to those with great power in the nation.

Interpreting the Scriptures

Judgments on the Surrounding Nations (1:3—2:5)

In the first two chapters, after a one-verse (1:2) introduction that identifies his message as one of impending doom coming from the Lord, Amos delivered messages of divine judgment on the small nations surrounding Israel. He was an inspired master preacher. Although we see his words today as a written message, they were delivered as an oral message.

Just imagine Amos proclaiming this message in the streets of Bethel or Samaria or any other settlement in Israel. In order, he condemned Syria, Philistia, Phoenicia, Edom, Ammon, and Moab before he got to Judah and Israel. If you will plot this on a map, you will see that a spiral pattern appears, moving from the outer edge to the center, which is Israel. Amos condemned each of these nations, using a poetic pattern:

"For three transgressions of _____, yea for four, I will not revoke the punishment." This is followed by their particular sins. "Therefore I will send fire on _____." Notice that the word "transgressions" is used. This translates a Hebrew word meaning willful, deliberate sin.

The use of "three . . . yea for four" probably is based on the Hebrew idea that seven indicates completion. Either it is three plus four equals complete involvement in transgression or when people move from three to four transgressions, they are well on their way to complete involvement in transgression.

The judgment in each case is by fire. Fire is a term frequently used for divine visitation, such as the judgment on Sodom and Gomorrah (Genesis 19:24).

Syria with its capital of Damascus was the first to be condemned (1:3–5). This nation was northeast of the Sea of Galilee. They had mistreated the people in Gilead, their Israelite neighbors just across their southern border, with cruel and inhuman practices.

The second oracle (1:6–8) condemned the Philistines, who lived on the Mediterranean seacoast southwest from Israel and Judah. The prophet mentioned four of the five major Philistine cities—Gaza, Ashdod, Ashkelon, and Ekron (Gath is omitted). They were condemned for selling captives as slaves to the Edomites.

Next he dealt with the Phoenicians, who lived along the coast north of Israel, with their capital at Tyre (1:9–10). They were also condemned for selling captives as slaves to the Edomites.

The fourth oracle of condemnation was directed against the Edomites (1:11–12). This, the brother nation to the Hebrews, was condemned for continual anger, hatred, and fighting directed against the Hebrews.

The Ammonites lived in the area east of the Jordan between the Hebrews who lived east of the Jordan River and the desert. They were condemned for the grossly inhuman practice of ripping open pregnant women to gain additional territory on their borders (1:13–15).

Next he addressed the Moabites (2:1–3), who lived to the east across the northern part of the Dead Sea. They were condemned for desecrating the bones of the Edomite king.

Then Amos pronounced divine judgment on the Kingdom of Judah (2:4–5)! There were differences in speech patterns between Judah and Israel, and it is almost certain that the hearers of Amos's words would know that he was from Judah. Even today among the Palestinians who live in this part of the world, the natives can identify the village from which people come by their speech. When Amos condemned his own people, the crowd he had gathered to hear him must have been convinced he was a true messenger from God. Judah was condemned for having rejected God's laws and statutes, following in the disobedient paths of their ancestors. Amos was now ready to deliver the major message he brought from the Lord to Israel.

A Longer, More Detailed Prophetic Oracle Condemning Israel (2:6–16)

2:6. Amos used the same beginning formula: "For three transgressions of Israel, and for four, I will not revoke the punishment; because. . . ." The Israelites were first condemned for oppression of the poor: righteous people were not valued for their righteousness; they were simply worth so much silver. One who was needy could be sold for the cost of a pair of sandals—an item of very little value.

2:7. The poor were merely trampled into the dust—or perhaps Amos pictured here the greed of the rich. The New King James Version translation is truer to the Hebrew—"They pant after the dust of the earth which is on the head of the poor." They were so land hungry that they lusted after the soil that fell as dust on the man's head! Can you imagine a more graphic picture of a rich man seeking more and more land? These rich, land-hungry Israelites were simply shoving any afflicted person out of their pathway.

"Father and son go in to the same girl, so that my holy name is profaned." The "girl" may be a cult or pagan temple prostitute or some other girl, perhaps a slave. The Hebrews have a word specifically for cult prostitute, but it is not used here. It may be, however, that a cult prostitute is implied by both the statement "so that my holy name is profaned," and the reference in the following verse to the "altar" and "the house of their god." At the very least the example and training that father provided for the son in such cases was an affront to a holy God.

2:8. "They lay themselves down beside every altar on garments taken in pledge." If this continues the preceding thought, as it must do, this encounter with the prostitute was at an altar, no doubt a pagan shrine. The floor, commonly made of dirt or stone, was carpeted with coats pawned by the poor. There are definite rules in the Old Testament concerning the pawning of clothing (see Exodus 22:26–27). With a total lack of concern for the poor, they used these pawned coats for carpet on the stone floors as they engaged in these immoral and drunken affairs in the name of religion!

2:9–11. This passage recounts what God had done for this people. He had destroyed the Amorites, a general name for the people residing in the land of Canaan when the Hebrews entered under Joshua. He had led them to escape from the power of the Egyptian Pharaoh and led them the forty years they spent in the wilderness and on to possess the land where they were now living. Then, after they had settled in the land, God continued to show them the right way to live, with the prophets to teach them and the Nazirites to show them by example. The prophets were those who brought the word of God. The Nazirites were those who took special vows to set an example for the people. They were to avoid anything produced by the grapevine, particularly wine; they were to allow no razor to touch their head, and they were to avoid any contact with a dead body (see Numbers 6). Apparently these vows were to remind their fellow Hebrews of the purer life they had in the wilderness before they were "contaminated" by contact with Canaanite culture and religion.

2:12. The response of the Hebrews to the direction and examples provided was almost violently negative. They forced the Nazirites to violate their vows by pouring wine down their throats. From the prophets they demanded silence when they should have been hearing the word of the Lord.

2:13–16. Divine judgment was surely to come on the faithless and rebellious Israelites. Verse 13 presents the graphic picture of an ancient farmer's cart. It was built of heavy rough-cut logs with solid stone discs for wheels, cutting deep ruts in the fields when it was loaded with ripened grain. So would God press Israel down in judgment. From God's judgment there would be no escape. Strength, might, weapons, speed of foot, even horses to ride—none or all of these would enable Israel to escape the just sentence of punishment from God.

Focusing on the Meaning

Amos addressed a contented, self-satisfied people who thought of themselves as God's special people. The audience would accept happily what

Amos said about the surrounding nations. But it was to the audience that his message was directed.

Remember that this lesson's text and meaning is directed to you and your class members. Too often the message of the Bible is understood to be directed to some other people, but remember that it was sent in the first place to God's own people. It is to us first, and then we can take it to others. It took conquest and loss of freedom, including exile to a foreign land, to persuade the Hebrews that God was speaking to them after all.

Through Amos's words, God directs us to have compassion for and to offer help to the poor. There are poor and needy people in every community in our land. It is easy to deny that this is our responsibility. But if we take seriously the teaching of the Bible—Old and New Testaments—we will recognize our responsibility. Were it not for the grace of God and the love of God we might be in their shoes—and we may be sometime.

The Hebrews needed to learn that Yahweh was the God of all of the nations. Amos set this out beyond a doubt as he spoke his messages concerning the surrounding nations. This lesson must call us again to recognize that God's concern goes far beyond the shores of the United States. He made all of the world; all of the peoples of the world are God's creation. All stand under God's judgment. All need to know of God's love and salvation. How can they hear if we do not tell them?

TEACHING PLANS

Teaching Plan—Varied Learning Activities

Connect with Life

1. Prior to the session enlist a class member to do the role-play representation found in step 10.

2. At the beginning of class write *A.C.T.S.* on the board. Ask whether anyone recognizes this acrostic as an approach to prayer. (Perhaps someone will identify the letters as standing for *Adoration, Confession, Thanksgiving, Supplication*.) Ask the class to think about which of these components of prayer seems to come more easily. Some may suggest adoration, or praising God; thanking God for

his blessings may come easiest to others. Point out that it seems we often rush to supplication because we have so many things to request of God.

3. Ask, *Which of the four components seems most difficult?* Someone will likely suggest confession as the hardest. Ask, *Why does confession come hardest?* Help class members address the reality that confession requires us to face our shortcomings. Suggest that we sometimes confess our sins in general but avoid dealing with specific ways in which we fail God and one another.

4. If you have a large world map available, display it. Pinpoint on the map, or write the names of these countries on the board: Colombia, Sudan, Iraq, Africa, North Korea, China. Point out that these are some countries with which the U.S. has had a "beef." Ask the class to name the issues we have with these countries (Columbia, drug trade; Sudan and China, human rights violations; Iraq and North Korea, weapons of mass destruction; Africa, rampant A.I.D.S. The class may be able to add to the list.) Then ask: *Does the United States have any of these problems? Which ones?*

5. Enlist someone to read aloud the Main Idea for today's lesson. Point out that Amos was addressing this very issue in the beginning of his prophecy.

Guide Bible Study

6. Divide the class into three groups. Ask the first group to search Amos 1:1; 7:14 and their *Study Guide* to find information that will help identify who Amos is. What inferences may be made from the information? Ask the second group to be prepared to report on what we know about Israel at the time of Amos (see the *Study Guide* lesson and introduction). Finally, ask the third group to observe Amos's technique of "working up" to his address to Israel. Point out that scanning Amos 1—2 will help with this assignment. If possible, have Bible commentaries available and encourage their use.

7. Ask for a report from the first group. Caution that it is important not to create an identity for Amos beyond what the Bible tells us. Point out, however, that Amos apparently was not a member of any professional religious group. In our parlance, we would call him a

"layman." What we do know for certain is that Amos was called by God to be God's spokesman to Israel.

8. Ask the second group to describe what they discovered about this period in Israel's history. Make the point that this was probably Israel's most prosperous period in their early history.

9. Ask the third group to report on their observations about Amos's technique for "working up" to his message to Israel. Be sure the group points out that Amos began with Israel's neighbors (note their locations as indicated in the *Study Guide*, or point them out on a map). Note that Amos got closer to home when he addressed their cousins, Judah. Then he zeroed in on Israel.

10. Invite eight volunteers to help visualize the scenario in today's passage. Assign one person to be Israel and stand in the middle of the group. Give each of the others one of the names of the nations included. As Amos 1:3—2:5 is read aloud, ask them to indicate through facial expressions the reaction of these nations to Amos's message (For example, the nation being addressed may appear angry or dismayed, perhaps remorseful. The others may be puzzled or simply ignore Amos. Israel will be smug, even gleeful, until he or she is addressed, at which point surprise, confusion or disgust may be expressed). You or an eighth volunteer then should read the indictment against Israel in 2:6–16. Point a finger at Israel to add accusation to the effect. (If your class is not large enough for this activity, simply invite someone to read the passage aloud and ask the class to consider how Israel might have been responding as it heard the messages.)

11. Allow the volunteers to be seated, and then ask, *What issues did God take up with Israel?* (Be prepared to point the class to verses 2:6–8.)

12. Lead the group to look at God's recounting of what God had done for Israel (2:9–12). Ask, *Is it safe to say that Israel had lost perspective on their own history?*

Encourage Application

13. Refer once again to the *A.C.T.S.* acrostic. Ask, *Thinking positively about our nation, how easy is it to praise God for God's goodness? What do we have to thank God for as a nation? How often do we ask God to*

bless and protect our nation? (If you have it, hold up one of the popular "God Bless America" bumper stickers). If appropriate, you may want to mention (or show if you can locate one) a bumper sticker with a different twist that has begun to appear: "America: Bless God." Discuss the meaning of this phrase.

14. Ask, *Do we have anything to confess as a nation?* Recall the "sins" of the nations with whom America contends. Ask, *Is it hypocritical for us to criticize others for issues we face here at home?* Refer to the small article in the *Study Guide* titled "The Sermon on the Mount." Ask, *How does this illustration apply to our nation?*

15. Challenge the group to discuss the *Study Guide* comments under "Implications for Today."

16. Close with the case study in the *Study Guide.* To facilitate discussion, divide the class into two or three smaller groups. Ask them to address briefly the questions included. After sufficient time for discussion, pose the questions one at a time and allow for random responses from any of the groups.

Teaching Plan—Lecture and Questions

Connect with Life

1. If a world map is available, display it in clear sight of the group. Write these words on the board: *extreme poverty; focus on class distinction; ethnic conflict; illicit drugs; human rights violations; economic corruption.* Ask, *Where in the world, outside the United States, are these issues a problem?* Place a red (or colored) sticker on the map as members offer suggestions. Then ask, *Does our nation have any of these problems? Which ones?*

2. Ask someone to read aloud the Main Idea and the Question to Explore.

Guide Bible Study

3. As you prepare to read today's Scripture, ask the class to listen for these things: *What does Scripture tell us about who Amos is? During*

what period in Israel's history did Amos deliver his message? Read Amos 1—2 aloud, or ask two people who read well to read one chapter each.

4. Ask, *What do we learn from Scripture about the person of Amos?* Point out that while we do not know much about Amos, there is no mention of his being a "preacher" or religious official. Suggest that in that regard, he is like us. It is clear, however, that he has been chosen by God to deliver God's message.

5. Ask, *What do we know about what was going on in Israel at this time?* In addition to the facts from Scripture, point out that this was apparently Israel's most affluent period in their history to date.

6. Ask the class whether they noticed anything interesting about the approach Amos took in getting the attention of his audience. Use question 3 from the *Study Guide*. Lead a brief discussion on this question to ensure that the group has a clear picture of the setting, including the rapport Amos was establishing here with his listeners.

7. Refer the class to Amos 1 and lead them to list the sins addressed by Amos. Put these verses on the board, and write the sin beside the verse as the class responds: 1:3, Aram (Damascus), apparent brutality; 1:6, Philistia (Gaza), capturing and selling people into slavery; 1:9, Tyre: selling people into slavery and breaking a treaty; 1:11, Edom, lack of compassion, unchecked anger; 1:13, Ammon, killing innocent women and children; 2:1, Moab, desecrating the bones of Edom's king; 2:4, Judah, failing to keep God's commands; 2:6–8, Israel, selling the righteous and the needy into slavery, mistreating the poor, denying justice to the oppressed, illicit sex, misappropriating resources.

8. Ask, *Against whom did the prophet enumerate the most sins? Why would Amos—actually God—be more concerned about the sins of Israel?* The obvious answer is that Israel was God's chosen! While the other nations may have pleaded innocence, Israel knew better! Yet they were so self-righteous.

9. Use the *Study Guide* comments to lead a discussion of the sins of Israel. Note that each sin seemed to have as its victim the poor, the downtrodden, the *have-nots*; in other words, those in society who had the least ability to defend themselves.

10. Point out that God showed both his disappointment and his anger in verses 9–11, when he reminded Israel of all he had done for them.

11. Ask the class to read in 2:13–16 how God planned to punish Israel for their sins. Invite volunteers to identify the specific punishments from each verse.

Encourage Application

12. "Bring the lesson home" by posing the questions from the *Study Guide*. Begin with question 4. Another way to frame that question is, *If Amos could have added one more nation to his list, if he had addressed the sins of America after he dealt with Israel, what would he say?* Proceed, as time allows, to use questions 1 and 2.

13. Conclude by asking the group to identify positive efforts in our culture to address the needs of the poor, the outcast, and the needy. If your church is involved in some of these, ask someone who has been involved to give a brief testimony. Challenge the class to find ways to become involved in and support specific ministries and services.

NOTES

1. "Qarqar," *New International Dictionary of Biblical Archaeology* (Grand Rapids, Michigan: Zondervan Publishing House, 1983), 375–376.

Focal Text

Amos 3:9—4:3; 5:10–15;
6:4–7; 8:4–6

Background

Amos 3:1—4:3; 5:1–17;
6:1–14; 8:4–14

Main Idea

God condemns economic
practices that mistreat the
poor and powerless.

Question to
Explore

Does God care about
economics?

Teaching Aim

To lead the class to
identify economic
practices that God
condemns and how these
apply to current life

A M O S

A God Who Roars

Lesson Two

Judgment on Injustice

BIBLE COMMENTS

Understanding the Context

Amos and his contemporaries lived in a world that was very different from our world. The Hebrews grew up in and valued the nomadic life-style that was practiced in the time of Abraham, Isaac, Jacob—their patriarch founders. After leaving Egypt and while in the wilderness, they were nomads. They looked back on this as the ideal way to live. Cooperation and sharing were absolute essentials for surviving in the desert. Basic needs were met by the entire community, working together and sharing openly with one another. This was not a socialistic society. There were private possessions, but there was generous sharing of the necessities of life. In the desert the land was to be used, but not possessed.

When the Hebrews entered the land of Canaan, for the very first time they were able to possess land on which they could live the year round without moving. So land was a treasured possession, not something to be bought and sold. Land was to be cared for diligently and passed on to future generations in good, fertile condition to provide a good life for them. The person who had no land was destined to a life of slavery in the Old Testament world. So the Old

21

Testament condemns land-grabbing. Even selling land was forbidden—except for that in cities with walls surrounding them (Leviticus 25)

The Hebrews were expected to hold the poor in high regard. Leviticus 25 directed their kinsmen to care for them without charge. The Year of Jubilee rules provided a means for the poor to regain ancestral property and once again become productive citizens. The economy of the Canaanites, in which both land and people were bought and sold, was very different from what the entering Hebrews had previously known. These new economic practices created many problems for the Hebrews. The poor were often oppressed, and problems with commercial activities became common. The poor and powerless were often pushed aside in the rush for riches and the material pleasures they provided.

Amos was not one to be silent about these issues. He saw Yahweh, their God, as having a great concern for every human being. Amos issued a clear call for justice and righteousness in every relationship in life.

Interpreting the Scriptures

The Coming Judgment (3:1—4:3)

3:1–8. The opening words of this passage indicate clearly that it is a word of judgment: it is spoken against the nation. Privilege carries with it responsibility. Israel had the privilege of knowing Yahweh; they could expect punishment for their failures to obey. We who know God's salvation through Christ are not free to sit back and enjoy our salvation. We have a responsibility to share our knowledge with the rest of the world.

In verses 3–6 the prophet asked seven questions, each of which has an obvious answer, leading up to verse 8, in which he stated that he absolutely must prophesy, for God had spoken. Here is an important truth about the prophets. They spoke, not because they chose to, or because someone asked them to, but because God's message revealed to them compelled them to speak. Jeremiah once decided that he would not speak God's message any more, but he could not be silent. He said that it became "like a burning fire shut up in my bones" (Jeremiah 20:9). Similarly, Amos felt compelled to deliver the message, for God had spoken

3:9–11. A courtroom scene is described in which witnesses were called from Philistia (Ashdod) and from Egypt to assemble in Samaria, the capital city of Israel, to witness and hear the charge God brought against an Israel filled with disturbances and oppressions. There was little or no peace and security. God's judgment that they did not know how to do right is a sad and devastating commentary on the city. The result was that violence and robbery abounded. Who would want to live in such a place? The judgment was, *Guilty*—and destruction would follow at the hands of an opposing nation.

3:12. The prophet pictured the coming destruction. Drawing on his experience as a shepherd, Amos likened the coming destruction of Samaria to the attack of a lion on a stray lamb. The shepherd, hearing the cries of the lamb, races to rescue it, but arrives to find no more than mere fragments of the animal. Only fragments of Samaria would survive.

3:13–15. The promised punishment would fall on the pagan religious establishment in the land and on those enjoying their ill-gotten wealth. Lest there be any doubt, Amos identified the source of his message as the "Lord God, the God of Hosts"—Yahweh, the commander of the heavenly hosts. Bethel was the location of the temple of the gold bull established by Jeroboam I about 922 BC when he led Israel to break away from Judah after the death of Solomon. Destruction was decreed for this altar. It evidently was completely destroyed. Archaeological excavations at Bethel have failed to reveal any trace of this temple or its altar.

The houses of the wealthy—who had summer as well as winter houses—were doomed. The reference to "houses of ivory" was puzzling for years, until archaeologists found carved ivory panels in the ruins of ancient Samaria—probably ivory panels adorning the outer walls of the houses of the very wealthy.

4:1–3. Amos condemned the luxury-loving women of Samaria. "Hear this word, you cows of Bashan." The word "cows" is the feminine form, and thus may be translated "heifers." Bashan was the area bordering Syria, east of the Sea of Galilee. It receives ample rainfall and has many small streams flowing through it. The cows of Bashan were always well-fed and satisfied. These women joined their husbands in oppressing the poor. They greedily called for their husbands to keep them well-supplied with wine. The prophet affirmed that the women shared the burden of guilt with their husbands for the oppression of the poor. They would share in the punishment to come. It is not a pretty picture that Amos painted for them. They would be taken away through the rubble of the broken-down walls with hooks. The reference is to the Assyrian practice of deportation. The Assyrians had a reputation in the ancient world for cruelty, especially in their treatment of captives. They tried to control a vast empire by deporting captive people far away from their homes. They hoped that people would less likely join a revolt in a strange land than in their native land. They transported thousands of captive peoples from their homelands to faraway places. Many (according to Assyrian records, 27, 290 people) were deported from Israel when it was conquered. "He carried the Israelites away to Assyria. He placed them in Halah, on the Habor, the river of Gozan, and in the cities of the Medes" (2 Kings 17:6). Then "the King of Assyria brought people from Babylon, Cuthah, Avva, Hamath, and Sepharvaim, and placed them in the cities of Samaria in place of the people of Israel." (2 Kings 17:24) One of the ways in which escapes were prevented while moving these large groups of people over long distances was to fasten them together with ropes and hooks. It is uncertain whether the prophet described removal of their bodies with hooks to throw them into "Harmon" (an unknown place) or marching the captives out, fastened together with hooks and ropes, to be taken to a place called Harmon.

A Corrupt System of Justice (5:10–15)

The gate of the ancient city was the only point of entry or exit of the city. The elders of a city would sit at the gate. They would gather there to see who was coming and going. Excavations in several ancient cities in Israel have uncovered rooms with low stone benches lining its walls, just inside the city gate. Soldiers would certainly be there in wartime, but likely in peacetime the elders would sit there. When a dispute arose in the city, the contesting parties would come to the gate, where the elders would serve as a local court. They would hear the evidence or complaints and render a decision. But Amos charged that the decisions were made on the basis of bribes paid to the elders. The truth was of no value. The poor had no chance of receiving justice in such a corrupt justice system. The corrupt judges had profited greatly. Their houses were of "hewn" stone—stone shaped and squared, rather than the common undressed field stone. Their houses were surrounded by "pleasant vineyards," but in God's righteous judgment, they would not benefit from either. The system of justice was so corrupt that silence was better than speaking the truth.

The key verse in this passage is verse 15: "Seek good and not evil, that you may live." It is the most hopeful note Amos has sounded up to this point. "Good" in the Old Testament refers to that which is in keeping with God's will, or that which God desires. The first time the word "good" appears in the Bible is in Genesis 1. When God called for light to come into existence, God saw that it was good. That means simply that it was exactly what God wanted. "Evil" is just the opposite: it is whatever is contrary to God's will. Seeking the good, or conforming one's life to the will of God, is the way to life.

Amos told the Israelites, *Do this and God will indeed be with you.* They had been falsely claiming God's presence. Amos promised that if they would seek that which pleases God, including bringing true justice into the gate-court, it might be that God would be gracious to "the remnant of Joseph." "Joseph," the father of Ephraim and Manasseh, two of the dominant tribes in its territory, is another way of referring to the Northern Kingdom, usually called Israel.

Here the prophetic concept of a remnant is first introduced. A remnant is a small, leftover part of something useful or valuable. The "remnant" in Amos is both a teaching of doom and one of hope. The fact that a mere remnant of the entire nation would survive was primarily doom, for the vast majority would not survive the disaster to come in judgment on the nation. But there was hope in the possibility that a few would survive the coming disastrous events.

Idle Luxury and Self-indulgence Faces Divine Judgment (6:4–7)

Amos drew a picture of the idle rich of his day. They lived in luxurious surroundings. Instead of working they lay about on beds decorated with costly ivory. They had choice foods—lambs from the flock or calves from the stall—where these animals would be fattened, producing tender, more desirable meat—rather than from the field, those producing tougher cuts of meat. Their songs were "idle," having neither encouraging nor uplifting qualities. They drank wine from bowls—perhaps referring to the quantity they consumed; bowls hold more than cups. Only the finest oils were used for rubbing on their skin. Oils were regularly used by the Hebrews for their skin, but these rich ones must have only the best. While they demanded the best for their personal pleasure, they had no concern for the downward slide of the nation. The "ruin of Joseph" may well refer to the economic, social, moral, political, and religious decay of the nation. Amos predicted that the rich would be among the first to be exiled to a strange land with nothing except the clothing they wore.

The Rich Riding Roughshod over the Poor (8:4–6)

Amos yet once more turned to the economic injustices in which the rich and powerful took advantage of and cheated the poor in the land of Israel. The picture of trampling on the poor is an appropriate description of the actions of the wealthy class. The oppressing merchant class was eager for the New Moon and Sabbath day to end so they could resume their dishonest practices. The New Moon, the first day of the month in the lunar calendar of the Hebrews, was a religious holiday, treated like the Sabbath (Num. 10:10; 28:11–15). The prophet charged them with using a smaller than standard container (a small ephah) for which they over-charged the customer (a great shekel).

The shekel was later the name of a coin, but at this time it was one of the "standard" weights for weighing the silver or gold used in purchases. Balance scales were used with stone weights. The shekel and other weights are frequently found in excavations today. They are smooth stones, flat on one side, usually marked with the weight by letters and symbols scratched into their rounded tops. With no enforcing of stan-dards, using false weights could easily have gone undetected by the poor of the land. These eager merchants were also condemned for buying the poor and needy for some silver or even a pair of sandals, a common and obviously cheap item. Their concern with profits rather than honesty is underscored by their practice of selling not only the wheat but also the trash or sweepings with the good wheat.

Focusing on the Meaning

Israel was given the undeserved gift of the knowledge of the one true God. A heavy responsibility went along with that gift. Their life as a nation must honor God and bear witness of him to the rest of the world. Amos pointed out how far they were from living by the laws God had given them. His message reminds us that our knowledge of the true God and of the Savior requires us to be faithful in our lives and our witness. We must avoid the arrogant attitude that our special relationship to God will somehow keep evil away from us.

The Hebrews—especially the wealthy—were guilty of oppressing and exploiting the poor. While the wealthy today revel in their pleasant and often extravagant life style, thousands in our land go to bed hungry nightly. We salve our conscience by passing the responsibility off on the "government." We have the privilege of positions in which we can be comfortable, even if not rich. It is not God's will that any should suffer from hunger. We cannot do nothing and be guiltless.

Amos set forth in clear terms that God demands that we live our lives conforming to God's will. That is what is good. Anything less than that is evil. We need to immerse ourselves in God's word to know God's will. As Christians we have the added advantage of the presence of the Spirit to guide us. But our part is to be obedient.

Even in the midst of abounding injustices and oppression and all kinds of evil, a loving God is ever seeking a way to redeem his rebelling creation. He expects us to let ourselves be used by him in this task.

TEACHING PLANS

Teaching Plan—Varied Learning Activities

Connect with Life

1. During the week prior to the session, call one of your members whom you know to be an internet user, and ask him or her to do some research on the amount spent on cosmetics in this country by both men and women. Ask the member to be prepared to make a brief report during class time. Pull from your Sunday paper the advertising circular section and take it with you to class. Make a montage on a focal wall of all of these ads by taping them randomly and at different angles, with overlapping edges and corners. As an alternative, simply spread them around on the floor at the front of the room or in the middle of the group.

2. Have two or three Bible commentaries on Amos available. Before the session, or as members assemble, enlist at least two people to accept these assignments: (1) research the meaning and identity of the "cows of Bashan" in Amos 4:1–3; (2) research the meaning of "hooks" and "fishhooks" from the same verses. Ask them to be prepared to report during the session.

3. Ask the following question at the beginning of the session: *What do we consider in this country to be the rewards of good upbringing, a good education, good health and hard work?* (Likely someone will mention making money.) Then ask: *When it comes to making money, how does one define "enough"?* Accept responses without comment.

4. Point out that it can be somewhat disconcerting when we find descriptions of ourselves or our own nation in Scripture. That is exactly what we find in Amos's contention with Israel.

5. Many in Israel had apparently become quite rich. Ask, *Is there anything wrong with being rich? When can being rich be a problem? When can it cause problems for others?* Point out the Question to Explore from the *Study Guide*: "Does God care about economics?" State that the answer is the focus of today's lesson.

Guide Bible Study

6. Point out that Amos spent much time and energy addressing the economic situation in Israel. Many were suffering at the hands of the affluent. Use the *Study Guide* comments on 3:9—4:3 to highlight the way God was going to deal with Israel. Call for reports from the people who researched "cows of Bashan" and "hooks" and "fish hooks." Lead the class to discuss the situation as described, being careful not to put all the blame on the women. The point, as applied both to the wives and their husbands, was their insatiable appetite for more.

7. Ask class members to work with a person seated next to them to explore 5:10–15 for what caused the disparity between the rich and the poor. After a few minutes of work, ask for reports (address the class as a group rather than ask each pair to report). Interpret the meaning of "in the gate."

8. Enlist someone to read 6:4–7 aloud. Suggest that the class listen for evidence of the great disparity between the rich and the poor in Israel. Call for responses, and add further details as needed.

9. Read 8:4–6 aloud and comment that Israel actually had instruction to do just the opposite of what we read here. Divide the class into thirds, and ask one third, in groups of three, to read Exodus 22:21–27; ask another third, in groups of three, to read Deuteronomy

16:11–12; the other third should read Deuteronomy 24:17–22. As they read they should look for the attitude Israel was supposed to have toward the poor. After several minutes of discussion call for comments from each of the larger groups.

Encourage Application

10. Ask *Are there places in today's passages where "America" could be substituted for Israel? Where, specifically?* Allow for several responses.

11. If you asked a member to do the pre-class research on the use of cosmetics in this country, call for a report at this time. Do not focus too much discussion here, as it is merely an illustration.

12. Ask the class to think of some visible evidence of our wealth, as well as our tendency to hoard our wealth. Allow for responses, but if they are not mentioned, include the growth of self-storage facilities throughout this country (you might pause to ask members to name the facilities in your own community, including when the newest was built). Then ask *How many of you have attics in your home? What do you keep in your attic?* You may then ask the following question: *How many of you have homes with a garage? What is in your garage?* Or, you might simply point out that many homes with garages have in them, not cars, but stuff! Ask, *How much food, how much clothing, how many homes, how much medicine and health care, do you suppose each of us or all of us together could provide for the poor of our country if we had not bought all the stuff we have stored?*

13. Have as many Bible concordances on hand as possible. Ask members to use these or the concordance in their Bible to look up both the word "rich" and the word "poor." Ask them to read down the list of entries for an idea of what each Scripture says about the word. Ask, *From the number of entries, and a brief reading of the short entries, what conclusions may we draw about God's attitude toward the poor?*

14. Comment that even in purchasing "necessities" (you might ask how we define "necessity") we must be responsible. Ask the class to form groups of three or four and read and discuss the *Study Guide* illustration about the Thai toy factory that burned.

15. Use as many of the questions from the *Study Guide* as time allows, but focus especially on question 1.

Teaching Plan—Lecture and Questions

Connect with Life

1. Begin by posing the question, *Does God care about economics?* Pause for several responses, and then follow with these questions: *WHAT does God care about economics? WHY does God care about economics?* Be prepared for several moments of silence while class members "process" these questions. If necessary, repeat the last question.

2. Remind the class that this session is the second in a series on the prophecy of Amos. He delivered a dire word of judgment on the nation of Israel. Refer to the Main Idea for the session. Enlist someone to read this statement aloud. Invite another person to read the Study Aim for the session.

3. Set the study in the context of Israel's history: during the days of the divided kingdom, when King Jeroboam II reigned. These were prosperous days for Israel, and many were enjoying the pleasures of such prosperity. Apparently, however, according to Amos's message, they were not carrying the responsibilities that such prosperity brings with it.

Guide Bible Study

4. Ask class members to turn to Amos 3:9—4:3. Ask the class to listen for these things as the Scripture is read: *What problem(s) had Israel's opulent living caused? What would be the consequences of Israel's inattention to these problems?* Enlist a member who reads well to read this passage aloud.

5. Explain the meaning of the "cows of Bashan" and the "hooks" and "fishhooks" in 4:1–3, using the *Study Guide* and "Bible Comments" in this *Teaching Guide*. Be careful not to lay all the blame on the wives, since both husbands and wives seemed intent on over-indulgence to the detriment of the poor.

6. Lead members to turn to 5:10–15 and read these verses silently, noting the ways the rich were making life difficult for the poor. Help the class understand the meaning of "in the gate" by reading Ruth 4:1. Clarify that the city gate was where legal cases were argued.

7. Point the class to 6:4–7. Ask the group to keep three images in mind as you read these verses: picture a homeless person, wrapped in a ragged coat, sleeping in a fetal position under a bridge; recall television images of overweight people crowding sidewalks as the news reports on obesity in this country; finally, picture yourself walking through the cosmetics department of a local department store. It may be helpful if you quickly write these three words on the board: *homeless, over-eating, cosmetics.*

8. Ask three people to turn to these passages, one each: Exodus 22:21–27; Deuteronomy 16:11–12; 24:17–22. Refer the rest of the group to Amos 8:4–6. Call for reading of the Exodus and Deuteronomy passages. Then read the Amos passage. Ask, *What is the contrast here?* Help the class see the discrepancy between the attitude with which Israel was supposed to treat the poor, and their actual behavior.

Encourage Application

9. Use the question posed in the *Study Guide*: *What does that have to do with us? What does that have to do with America?* Write such names as these on the board: Enron, Worldcom, Tyco, ImClone. Ask, *What do these words have in common?* (companies under investigation for corruption) Invite class members to add to the list.

10. Refer to the statistics in the *Study Guide* under "Great Disparity Between Rich and Poor." Ask for other illustrations, both nationally and locally. Write these statistics from the U.S. Census Bureau on the board: Over the past two years the poverty rate in America has continued to rise: for children, 16.3 percent; for people ages 18–64, 10.1 percent; total in poverty in this country, 32.9 million in 2001. State this question in your own words: *While we could point the finger of blame in many directions, what is our personal responsibility to the poor around us?*

11. Close by asking the class to name local programs that address the needs of the poor. If members are involved with these groups, allow them to give a brief testimony about their involvement. Encourage members to find ways to make a personal contribution through action.

Focal Text

Amos 4:4–5; 5:18–24

Background

Amos 4:4–13; 5:18–27

Main Idea

God abhors hypocritical religious ceremonies, calling instead for justice in human relationships.

Question to Explore

Is worship the most important task of the church?

Teaching Aim

To help the class identify ways in which their worship practices may be hypocritical and decide to view them as God does

A M O S

A God Who Roars

Lesson Three

Judgment on Religious Hypocrisy

BIBLE COMMENTS

Understanding the Context

In Old Testament times Israel lived in a world with two great power centers. Egypt was on the south. Egypt's golden age when with splendor it ruled much of the ancient world was now in the past. Yet Egypt was still a formidable power. Since Egypt felt that Canaan was necessary for its own defense, Egypt continued to involve itself in Canaan's affairs. The other great power center was in the river valley usually called Mesopotamia, where the Tigris and Euphrates rivers flowed to the Persian Gulf. There Assyria, in the previous century an aggressive force, was now a sleeping giant, soon to awaken and swallow the small kingdom of Israel. Israel constantly had to reckon with both of these great powers. Amos came in a time when both were weaker than usual and were causing little trouble for Israel.

In this opportune time Israel had grown to its greatest strength as a separate nation, ruled over by Jeroboam II. It was a time of peace and prosperity—at least for the rich. No threats appeared on the horizon, and a self-satisfied people went through the formal motions of religion but without sincerity or personal devotion. The formalities of religion were there, but it went no more than skin deep, if that far. The previous lesson dealing with the economic injustices rampant in the land points to the lack of serious religious devotion among the people of Israel. Here we will look at the way in which the Israelites practiced their religion—often with serious hypocrisy.

Interpreting the Scriptures

Much Worship; Little True Commitment (4:4–5)

Bethel and Gilgal were both important religious centers in Israel. Bethel, in Hebrew meaning "house of God," first appears in the biblical story as a place where Abraham camped for a time (see Genesis 12:8). It had an important place in the story of Jacob's fleeing from the wrath of Esau. There he slept and dreamed of the ladder to heaven on which the angels were descending and ascending (Gen. 28:10–19). Back to Bethel he went in a serious religious experience after he returned to Canaan (Gen. 35). Bethel was one of the two places where Jeroboam I had built temples after he led the northern tribes to break away from Judah after Solomon's death (1 Kings 12:29). Many scholars think that Bethel was the scene of all or most of Amos's prophesying. It was perhaps the most important religious place in the kingdom of Israel.

Five different places are called Gilgal in the Bible. The most important and very likely the one mentioned here was between Jericho and the Jordan River. There the Hebrews camped after crossing the Jordan as they prepared for the battle of Jericho (Joshua 4:19–24). Apparently the tabernacle (the movable temple constructed by the Hebrews in the wilderness) remained there until the Hebrews completed their battles for the land (Josh. 18:1). At least into the eighth century BC Gilgal remained an important religious center among the Hebrews. Hosea, a near contemporary of Amos, also mentioned Gilgal as a center of sacrifice (Hosea 4:15; 9:15; 12:11). Amos mentioned Gilgal again in Amos 5:5.

In a statement that is clearly sarcastic, Amos called the people to go to Bethel and to Gilgal to transgress and multiply transgressions. The clear implication is that at these places of worship sacrifices were being offered, but the worship was insincere. Instead of atoning for sin, the worship activities were actually compounding transgression. Transgression was deliberate sin. This sin could not be atoned for by sacrifice. People guilty of this deliberate kind of sin could only cast themselves on the mercy of

God and beg for forgiveness. Instead of atoning for sin and pleasing God, their superficial and insincere worship at these places was adding to their burden of guilt before God.

Amos accused the people of being super-religious but completely false or insincere in it all. One was not expected to bring a sacrifice every morning or tithes every three days. Offerings of leavened bread were not expected. Freewill offerings were exactly that—never required. The Israelites of Amos's time obviously loved worshiping but didn't love God. Love for worship leads to more of the same kind of worship. Love for God results in changed lives and humble service in God's name.

Prepare to Meet Your God (4:6–13)

Seven catastrophic warnings were sent to the nation. All were ignored. The first was famine. Note the picturesque way it is described: "I gave you cleanness of teeth" (4:6). There was not enough food to get their teeth dirty. Then came a scorching drought (4:7–8). Next their crops were ravaged by blight and mildew (4:9). The locust then came and devoured even the trees (4:9). The fifth was a pestilence reminding them of the plagues that fell on Egypt (4:10). Then came a devastating military defeat in which their choice young men were killed (4:10). Finally there was the visitation of destruction like that which fell on Sodom and Gomorrah (4:11). In warning after warning, God said through the prophet, "Yet you did not return to me" (4:11). Then came the conclusion that should have chilled the unrepentant sinner: "Prepare to meet your God" (4:12).

Who is this God they must face? His incomparable might and greatness is proclaimed in 4:13. It is one of several majestic doxologies, songs of praise to God, that Amos gives. The One you must prepare to meet is the same One who created the mountains and the winds. It is amazing that such a One chooses to reveal his thoughts to mere human beings. He makes "the morning darkness" and walks "on the heights of the earth." Who is he? Yahweh, the God who commands the heavenly host, is his name!

Amos marveled at the truth that such a mighty God would stoop to have concern for lowly human beings. The concerned love God has for people is the central theme of the Scriptures, both Old and New Testaments.

The Darkness of the Day of the Lord (5:18–20)

In this passage Amos introduced the concept of the Day of the Lord as a day of God's righteous judgment, a theme that will be seen frequently in later prophets. In the popular religion among the Hebrews in Amos's time, the Day of the Lord was considered to be a great day and was eagerly anticipated. *After all*, they said, *we are God's chosen people. We should have and certainly will have dominance over all the other people of the world. Did not our God teach the mighty Pharaoh a lesson or two for mistreating us? We can hardly wait for God to move against all these who oppose us today. The Day of the Lord will be a great day when we will be set in our rightful place, dominating all these who now plague us.*

In their thought the Day of the Lord would be the day when God intervened in human history. They, as God's chosen people, would be exalted to world dominance. Any who opposed them would face disaster. Far from their thought was the fact that they also would face the righteous judgment of God.

Amos set the record straight: *Do you think you are ready to face the righteous judgment of God?* He pictured that day as dark and gloomy, with no light, no brightness in it.

Amos reminds us that we must face this awe-inspiring righteous God as judge one day. The wonderful truth of the New Testament is that we have God's Son to stand with us, to share with us his righteousness and to testify that he has atoned for our sins on the cross.

In a graphic picture Amos described this day as inescapable. A man out somewhere alone is met by a lion. Somehow he manages to escape the attack of this feared beast only to run into a bear. (Yes, there were lions and bears in ancient Israel.) Now this man is doubly fortunate in managing to escape from the bear. He then, safely he thinks, runs into his house and leans in exhaustion against the wall. But a serpent crawls from a crack in the wall, strikes his hand resting on the wall, and the man falls dead on the spot. (The "or went into the house" in the NRSV and other translations should read "and went . . . ," as the Hebrew text does.) No matter what you do, how hard you try to avoid it, you and each fellow human being will one day face a righteous God who will sit in judgment on each one.

Israel's Unacceptable "Worship" (5:21–23)

Worship is something we offer to God. He, not the one worshiping, must be the center of worship. Large sections of the Old Testament are given to descriptions of proper and appropriate worship of Yahweh. Amos went down a list of worship activities among his contemporaries: festivals, solemn assemblies, burnt offerings of animals, grain offerings, peace offerings, songs, and instrumental music. These God hates, despises, rejects.

The Hebrews celebrated several festivals during the year. The most common was the Sabbath, remembering God as creator. It was celebrated every seventh day. It was affirmed in the Ten Commandments (Exodus 20:8–11).

The next most common was the New Moon festival, the first day of each month. The Hebrews used a lunar calendar; so this was celebrated every twenty-nine to thirty days (Numbers 28:11–15).

There were four annual festivals. Perhaps the most prominent was Passover, celebrating the deliverance of the Hebrews from Egyptian slavery. It was celebrated in March—April (see Ex. 12—13; Leviticus 23:4–14). Pentecost or Weeks was a harvest festival, celebrating the spring grain harvest, coming fifty days after Passover (Ex. 34:22; Lev. 23:15–22). The fall harvest festival, celebrated after all the crops were gathered, was called the feast of Ingathering or Booths or Tabernacles (Ex. 23:16, Lev. 23:39–43). It was celebrated by living in booths or tabernacles—a temporary shelter—for the seven days of the festival. Each of these harvest festivals celebrated God as provider for the physical needs of his people. The Day of Atonement was the most solemn of the annual festivals. It was a day of confession and atonement for sins. It was the one day when the high priest was permitted to enter the holy of holies in the temple. There he made atonement for the sins of the nation before the mercy seat atop the ark of the covenant (Lev. 16). This festival celebrated God as redeemer and forgiver of his people.

Evidently these festivals had been stripped of their religious meaning and had become mere celebrations in the time of Amos. As such they were not pleasing to God. The same condemnation was pronounced on the sacrificial offerings of the Israelites. Leviticus 1—7 gives a detailed description of the various offerings the Hebrews were to present to God. In his condemnation of their hollow religious practices, Amos mentioned three of these—the burnt offering (an animal sacrifice; Lev. 1:1–17), the grain offering (Lev. 2:1–16), and the peace, "well-being," or freewill offerings (Lev. 3:1–17). These, as practiced by Amos's contemporaries, were totally unacceptable to God.

Music was an important part of the worship of the Hebrews. The Old Testament refers to various instruments—bells, cymbals, harps, lyres, flutes, pipes, horns, trumpets, tambourines, and especially the *shofar* or ram's horn. The Book of Chronicles gives much information about

David's arrangement of musicians for the temple services. Probably many of the psalms were sung in worship. In the false and superficial worship in this time, this "music" was only raucous noise in God's ear, not the joyful noise in which God delights.

The Answer: Justice and Righteousness (5:24)

God was not pleased with the festivals, sacrifices, and songs of the people pretending to worship. They went through all of the proper motions but without any sincerity or personal involvement. But Amos continued, telling his contemporaries exactly what God desired: justice and righteousness.

Justice is that which is right and true, that which has been determined just and correct both by God's law and by human experience in legal decisions of the past and in the lives of God's people. Righteousness means much the same, but its emphasis is on what has measured up to the divinely-set standard and so is undeniably the correct standard for human conduct.

Amos addressed not only the needed qualities of justice and righteousness but also the quantities of these desired. Let them roll down in abundance like waters, like waters in a perennial stream. In Israel very few streams flow year round. Most are called *wadis*—riverbeds with water only in the rainy season, and then usually only when it has rained in the area. A perennial stream has great and abundant life-giving potential. The prophet called for righteousness and justice in consistent abundance.

If there is only one verse you remember from Amos, this should be the one. More than any other, Amos 5:24 sums up his message—justice, righteousness, every day, every night, and in overflowing abundance.

Focusing on the Meaning

Some of Jesus' strongest criticisms were directed to hypocrites. They were those who pretended to do one thing and did another. They were only "play-acting" in their religion. A term of derision we often use for them is "two-faced." The same person shows one face to one and a different face to another. We dislike hypocrisy, and we must not let it slip into our lives and worship. We must have the same values and attitudes on Sunday and all the other days of the week.

Worship is directed to God; it is to please and honor God. Is our worship to please or entertain the people gathered, or is it to honor, adore, and please an Almighty God?

It is fine to enjoy worshiping, but enjoyment is not its purpose. The word "worship" in our English Bibles usually translates a Hebrew word meaning to bow down or prostrate oneself. God was not pleased with the worship in Amos's time. We need to be certain that our worship pleases God.

Whether we live until the Lord chooses to return and bring the end or we die before that time, we each must face God. None of us can know exactly when that will be. Amos's message about the "Day of the Lord" reminds us of the certainty that we will stand before God—a holy, righteous God—with our sin-stained lives. As Amos put it: "Prepare to meet your God" (4:12).

TEACHING PLANS

Teaching Plan—Varied Learning Activities

Connect with Life

1. *Prior to the session:* Collect several copies of your church's order of worship (for the current Sunday if possible) if you plan to use step 12. Check the hymnal used by your church for a responsive reading on worship. Be prepared to use this responsive reading to close today's session. Enlist two volunteers to conduct the role play at the end of this teaching plan. Encourage them to ad-lib appropriately to make the role play believable.

2. Begin by asking, *What is your favorite part of worship in our church?* Allow for responses, and encourage participants to explain their responses. Share your own response as well.

3. Lead class members to think through your worship service and name the elements of the order of worship. Then ask, *Why do you think we follow this particular order in our worship?*

4. Ask, *How would you characterize the style of worship in our church?* Some will probably recall the current labels given to various styles: traditional, contemporary, blended. If not, suggest these as possible choices, and ask which describes your worship. Then ask, *Do you think God really cares about the style of our worship? What might be more important to God than style?*

Guide Bible Study

5. Remind your class that this is the third lesson in a series from Amos, which examines the charges God brought against Israel. First was the charge of focusing on the sins of others instead of their own. Then Amos addressed Israel's treatment of the poor (getting rich at the expense of the poor). In today's lesson Amos turns to their practice of worship, or more accurately, God's dissatisfaction with their worship.

6. Divide the class into two research groups. Give these assignments:
    Group 1—Read Amos 4:4–5. Examine the meaning and significance of the sarcasm used in these verses by using and discussing the comments on this passage in the *Study Guide*.
    Group 2—Read Amos 5:18–24. Using the *Study Guide*, look for answers to these questions:

    • What is the meaning of "the day of the Lord"?
    • What elements of Israel's worship did God reject?
    • What feasts did the Israelites observe?
    • What was God really looking for from Israel?

7. After adequate time for research and discussion (about fifteen minutes), call for reports.

8. Ask, *What seemed to be Israel's greatest problem in their worship and religious practice?* (They were more concerned about their orders of worship and rituals than about their *attitudes* of worship and about right living—ensuring the justice that God requires.)

Encourage Application

9. Ask, *How pure are our motives when we come to worship? What are some distractions we encounter when we approach worship?* Allow for a

few responses. Then without introduction, cue the role players enlisted earlier to begin their monologues.

Role Play

One person will be a worship leader, the other a worshiper. The players should feel free to ad-lib appropriately.

Worship leader (as if projecting to the congregation): Welcome all who come with open hearts to worship God in spirit and in truth.

Worshiper (in a hushed tone): Shish! I thought I would never find a parking place. I had to walk so far that now I'm exhausted.

Worship leader: Oh God, we come with thankful hearts, to give ourselves in worship, to honor you as the one true, living God, to praise you as the Creator of all that is.

Worshiper: Good grief! Look at that outfit she's wearing! Where in the world did she get that!

Worship leader: As we join together in singing this new song, notice the attributes of God it acknowledges, and make this your heartfelt praise.

Worshiper: Where in the world do they find these new songs? Why can't we just sing the old songs that don't even require a hymn book!

---

10. Point out that much conflict in churches today occurs over preferences about worship styles. Ask, *Who is the audience in true worship? Which do you think is more important to God—the style of worship or the attitude of the worshipers?*

11. Depending on available time, you may need to adjust how to use this step and steps 12 and 13. Use the case study in the *Study Guide*, and close with step 12. Or continue with steps 12 and 13.

12. Distribute copies of the order of worship for today's worship. Lead the class to consider why each element of worship is included by using questions such as these: *Why do we have a "call to worship"? Why do we sing hymns? Why take an offering? Why do we have a sermon?*

Why do we have an "invitation"? Then ask, *What is the individual worshiper's role in each of these elements?*

13. Close by reading together the responsive reading you selected concerning worship. Challenge class members to consider their personal attitudes toward worship as they enter the sanctuary today.

Teaching Plan—Lecture and Questions

Connect with Life

1. Ask class members to recall their earliest memory of worship, perhaps as a child. *What, specifically, do they recall? Throughout their memories of worship, what have they looked forward to most? Why has this been important to them?*

2. Ask whether class members ever consider the reason for the order of worship your church follows. Allow discussion of your church's worship, but be cautious not to let discussion degenerate into a gripe session. Keep the tone positive.

3. Point out that in today's lesson, we see that Israel practiced very elaborate worship. Yet Amos delivered a severe judgment from God: their worship stank! It was not that they had the *order* wrong; it was that they worshiped with the wrong *attitudes*.

Guide Bible Study

4. Encourage class members to turn to Amos 4:4–5. Ask them to listen for the sarcasm in these verses as God taunted Israel concerning their worship. Read these verses with a tone of sarcasm. Explain the locations of the shrines and their significance. Point out that the last comment in verse 5 suggests that they loved the practices of worship more than they loved something else much more important to God. What could that be? (a rhetorical question; the answer will be revealed later) Elaborate as needed on the selfish attitude with which Israel apparently approached worship.

5. Suggest that the class read silently 5:18–20. Ask, *What is the meaning of "the day of the Lord"?* Refer to the small article, "The Day of the Lord," in the *Study Guide* to explain this concept, pointing out the difference between Israel's expectation and what God said would be the reality.

6. Enlist a member to read 5:21–24 aloud, pausing briefly after each line. As the verses are read, write on the board the elements of Israel's worship that God rejected: religious feasts and solemn assemblies; sacrifices and offerings; songs. Ask, *What were the feasts Israel observed?* Allow for responses, filling in information as needed, including the significance of these observances to the Israelites. Note that God even stopped his ears against their music!

7. Verse 24 gives a clear reason why God rejected Israel's worship. Lead the class to read the verse and look for what it says about what God desires more than anything else (justice and righteousness). Recall from the previous two lessons the issues God had with Israel: self-righteousness and injustice to the poor! No worship, however elaborate, was acceptable in light of these sins!

Encourage Application

8. Use these questions to guide discussion: *How often have you heard someone comment critically about our worship services? Who is the audience in worship? Is worship supposed to entertain us or to be directed toward God?*

9. Put a rating scale on the board like this:

   Low   1   2   3   4   5   6   7   8   9   10   High.

   Ask, *If God were to use a rating scale for our worship, how do you think it would rate?* State that perhaps a better question would be, *How would our worship attitude rate?* Allow for discussion, but guard against inappropriate criticism. Under no circumstances allow discussion to become personal.

10. Use question 1 from the Study Guide: *What kind of worship do you think God enjoys?*

11. Close by reading the Atlanta pastor's story about the young woman who attended worship for the first time.

Focal Text

Amos 7:7–17

Background

Amos 7:1—8:3

Main Idea

Obeying God is to take precedence over all else.

Question to Explore

What happens when religion gets cozy with government?

Teaching Aim

To lead the class to identify ways of hearing and obeying God's message in the midst of current culture

A M O S

A God Who Roars

God's Message Rejected

BIBLE COMMENTS

Understanding the Context

The nation of Israel was plunging headlong to keep its appointment with disaster. Their king, Jeroboam II, was an able political ruler, even expanding the territory of his kingdom. There was, for the most part, a peaceful coexistence with the other nations around Israel. He was an astute ruler who managed the affairs of state with a good sense of world politics in the arena of his world. How else could he have survived for forty-one years on a throne that had eighteen other kings who, on average, lasted only eight to nine years each? About his religious life and leadership we only know that the biblical historian reports that "he did what was evil in the sight of the Lord" (2 Kings 14:24). Important in this condemnation was the fact that he continued to support the religious practices established by Jeroboam I at Bethel and probably at other places as well. The king continued to control the royal temples at Bethel and Dan.

Barring a radical change in the lifestyle of the nation and a return to Yahweh, Amos saw no hope for the nation, at least for the short term. Eventually he would express some hope for the long-term future. In our background passage the prophet described five visions God had sent to him. Each one was quite different, but each predicted catastrophic doom for the nation and its people.

The Book of Amos gives no hint of how these visions were disclosed to him, whether by dreams or other means. But Amos clearly affirmed that the Lord showed him these things. As he met with God on these occasions, he responded to God with intercession for the people. God was sometimes persuaded. But the overwhelming final message is one of disaster to befall the nation.

At least this part of Amos's prophetic preaching was in Bethel, the city where the temple with a gold bull had been in operation since the break with the descendants of David in 922 BC. In the absence of both ancient descriptions and archaeological remains, we assume that the temple in Bethel was similar to other known temples from the eighth century BC. There, as in most temples of the time, worship centered on sacrifices burned on an outdoor altar. There was probably an indoor place to burn incense. Central to the temple would have been an image set up near the altar. In this case the image was that of a bull of cast metal overlaid with gold.

Some interpreters have argued that when Jeroboam I originally built this shrine at Bethel as well as the one at Dan (1 Kings 12:28–33), he intended that the gold calf or bull serve as a throne or seat for the invisible Yahweh, much as the ark of the covenant did in the Jerusalem temple. We are unable to fathom what was in the mind of Jeroboam I back in 922 BC. It is difficult to imagine a poorer choice than a bull for Yahweh to sit on, however, especially in this land where the great competitor with Yahweh for the devotion of the people was Baal, usually symbolized by a bull.

Interpreting the Scriptures

Four Visions of Impending Judgment (7:1–9; 8:1–3)

Chapter 7 begins with three visions, all stated in very similar terms, but the action and details of each differ. The pattern is:

> This is what the LORD God showed me.
>   The vision follows.
> The prophet intercedes for the condemned nation.
>   In visions one and two, God relents, but not in vision three.

The first vision (7:1–3). The first vision was of locusts beginning to appear just as the second growth of the hay crop was emerging. This was a critical time for the farmer. The king had required the first mowing of the fields as tax revenue. Only what grew later belonged to the farmer. Now it appeared that there would be nothing left for the farmer. But upon Amos's appeal, God relented and did not send the locusts.

The second vision (7:4–6). The second vision was of God calling for a shower of fire that devoured "the great deep" and was eating up the land. The picture is of a searing drought in which the water sources dried up and the land was burned. Amos again begged God to relent, which God did.

The third vision (7:7–9). The third vision was of God standing with a plumb line in his hand beside a wall. The word in the Hebrew text appears nowhere else in the Bible, and it primarily means lead (the metal). In this vision it was a lead weight, or plumb bob. A plumb line consists of a string tied to a plumb bob—a heavy, balanced weight, usually shaped like a child's top. When the bob is dropped, the force of gravity will cause the attached string to hang perfectly upright from the earth. Such a device has been used through the centuries to prevent leaning walls or buildings. The plumb line can always be counted on to give an absolutely straight, upright wall. The message to Amos was that God had a plumb line in the midst of Israel. God has an absolute standard of justice and righteousness. Did Israel measure up? Obviously Israel did not. The announced judgment of doom was on the places of pagan worship, the high places and sanctuaries in the land. They were to be made desolate. God also promised to rise against the house of Jeroboam with the sword.

The fourth vision (8:1–3). A fourth vision is recorded at the beginning of chapter 8. In this vision the Lord showed Amos a basket of summer fruit. When the Lord inquired as to what Amos saw, his response was, "a basket of summer fruit." God's response was to say, "The end." This vision seems strange to us, but to the reader of the Hebrew text, it is obviously a play on words or a pun. When Amos responded to tell what he saw, he said *qayits* (summer fruit). God responded, *Qayts* (the end). This sort of literary pun or word play is not unusual in Hebrew. It was an ear-catching way of presenting a message in a way that could be remembered. No more was the divine punishment to be delayed. The end had come. The temple songs would become laments. The many dead bodies cast out suggests that there would be too many to bury. The result: be silent; be quiet and wait on the Lord.

Confrontation with Amaziah (7:10–17)

7:10–11. Amaziah, the priest at Bethel, probably appointed by the king, was disturbed by the messages of Amos. When Amos said that God would rise against the house of Jeroboam with the sword, Amaziah sent a message to King Jeroboam II, who lived in Samaria. Amaziah charged Amos with mounting a conspiracy against the king. The message Amaziah reported as coming from Amos does not appear in Amos's recorded oracles. Amos either delivered messages in addition to those recorded in his book or Amaziah was fabricating a message to persuade the king to move against the prophet who was critical of the Bethel temple. According to Amaziah, who was probably quoting Amos correctly, Amos had predicted a violent death for Jeroboam and exile for the nation.

7:12–13. Sending a message to the king was not enough for Amaziah. He came out to confront the prophet personally. Imagine Amos in the simple garb of a shepherd facing Amaziah in the splendid robes of the priest of a royal sanctuary. Haughty and with biting sarcasm, the impressive-appearing priest demanded: "O seer, go home to Judah, earn your bread there, and prophesy there—never again at Bethel—this is a royal sanctuary" (7:12, writer's translation). Note first that Amaziah called Amos a "seer," not a prophet. Sometimes these words are used interchangeably, but "seer" emphasizes one who sees visions, while *prophet* emphasizes one who speaks a message from God. When Amaziah told Amos to eat bread in Judah, he was accusing Amos of prophesying for pay—for bread.

7:14–15. Amos was challenged, and he rose to the occasion. Here he responded with that meager information about himself that was mentioned in our first lesson on Amos. When he responded that he was not a prophet, he was denying that he was a professional prophet. That is, he was not one who made his living by prophesying. Very often in the ancient world a son followed in the occupation of his father. So Amos pointed out that neither was his father a prophet. God took him from his work as shepherd and dresser or pruner of sycamores and sent him to prophesy.

7:16–17. Amos then turned to speak a specific message concerning Amaziah and his family, predicting disasters for all of the family. His children were to be killed and his wife would become a prostitute when the city was conquered. Death in exile was in store for the priest himself when Israel was taken away from her land. The specifics of these disastrous events in store for this family are those commonly occurring during and after a war in which a nation was captured and taken to exile. Similar cruel events were in store for the other families of the rebellious nation who had turned away from their covenant faith.

Historically Baptists have held adamantly to the concept and practice of separation of church and state. Problems are almost certain to arise when these two are joined together. Typical problems are illustrated here. Amaziah was the official priest at an official temple. He was a part of the governmental administration of the nation, Israel. Had he chosen to do so, he was not in a position to call the king to account for his sinful and unethical deeds. As a part of the government of the king, he was a part of the religious problem afflicting the nation. Religious leaders need to be free not only to worship according to the dictates of their consciences, but also to criticize moral and ethical weaknesses and failures wherever they are found, in the government or elsewhere. A religious leader must be free to represent God and God's message to people without filtering it through any governmental or other human agency.

Amaziah did not represent God. Instead he represented self-interest and the king's interest. The people of Bethel were faced with competing claims to their religious devotion—Amaziah or Amos. The early followers of Jesus in Jerusalem also faced such a dilemma when the Sanhedrin, the Jewish body in charge of the temple, ordered them to speak no more in the name of Jesus (Acts 5:27–29). Their response was, "We must obey God rather than any human authority." Amos chose to obey God. We are called to follow his example.

Focusing on the Meaning

I have never experienced a vision like those Amos reported, and probably you have not either. I have, however, had clear understanding of God's direction in my life. We need to keep our lives in tune with God so that we can perceive God's will and guidance in our lives. God used Amos to point out wrongs in the land of Israel and to give guidance to the godly way for the nation. God still works through people, common people like Amos, only a common shepherd and sycamore pruner, to point out the wrongs to avoid and the godly way for the nation. Whatever your abilities, devoted to God, you can make a difference today.

Religion can easily become "what we do in church." Amaziah saw religion as what went on under his direction in the temple at Bethel. Religion, however, is a relationship with God. It has roots in and takes direction from our worship, which is often done best in church. But if that is the totality of our religious experience, we have misunderstood. We must live each day in the light of a faith commitment to God through Christ.

God's plumb line is still in use. His standards of justice and righteousness have not changed. We need to ask ourselves, *How do I measure up beside God's plumb line? How does our nation measure up?* Our nation was shocked into a greater religious awareness and worshiping God by the catastrophic events of September 11, 2001, but that religious devotion and awareness quickly faded to the previous level of complacency in only a few months.

Our God is a patient God. In the visions of Amos, twice God withheld judgment on his rebellious people. As Amos saw it, there is an end to God's patient love, however. Never confuse God's patience with complacency on his part. He promises that every knee will bow before him and every tongue will confess that Jesus Christ is Lord (Philippians 2:10–11). For some that will come too late. Remember that God has called us not only to worship him, but to be God's witnesses in all the world.

TEACHING PLANS

Teaching Plan—Varied Learning Activities

Connect with Life

1. *Prior to the session:* Secure a plumb line, perhaps from a friend's workshop. Have the plumb line handy for a demonstration at the beginning of the class session.

2. Also prior to class, enlist four class members to participate in an informal debate on this proposition: *Baptists' historical position on separation of church and state was appropriate in the simpler times of our nation's beginning. However, it is no longer practical due to the*

complexities of our world, the moral/ethical dilemmas our leaders face, and their need for spiritual guidance. Appoint two to the "pro" position, and the other two to the "con." Assure the volunteers that you will explain to the class that the positions debaters take are not necessarily their own but are meant to stimulate discussion and examination of the issue. Explain to the debaters that they will have three minutes each to state their positions and their rebuttals. The purpose is not to resolve the issue but to stimulate discussion.

3. At the beginning of class show the plumb line and ask someone to identify it. Ask for explanations of its use (such as laying bricks or stones; aligning walls and door frames; setting posts). Demonstrate the use of the plumb line by holding it up to the edge of the chalk or marker board to determine whether the board is hung straight. Check the facing of the door to your classroom. Look for other things around the room to check using the line.

4. Tell this incredible but true story: Not too many years ago a prominent building in a large city was under construction, with an external elevator shaft running up the outside of the building's front. Walking toward the new building one day, an employee of the business owning the building thought he noticed that the shaft under construction, now several hundred feet high, seemed to be leaning in one direction. Interrupting one of the workmen, the two men walked a block away, turned and assessed the tower. Indeed the tower was several degrees out of line, bowed to the right! Had the tower been completed and an elevator installed, it probably would never have worked properly. The shaft had to be demolished and reconstructed! Apparently the builders had neglected to use a centuries old, but very useful tool—a plumb line!

5. Ask, *What is our plumb line for gauging right living?* (Scripture). Point out that today we examine God's word to see how God used a plumb line to compare Israel's actions with his teachings.

Guide Bible Study

6. Point out that today's passage contains four visions of Amos. Ask members to read 7:1–3 and look for the first vision. Call for a description of this vision. Then ask, *What was Amos's response to the vision? What was God's response to Amos?*

7. Encourage members to read 7:4–6. Ask the same questions as in step 5.

8. Then ask members to read 7:7–9. Ask, *What was the vision? What was Amos's response?* (He was silent!) Then ask, *What was the purpose of the plumb line God said he was going to use?* State that Amos may have been silent this time because he knew Israel was not being obedient and would not measure up to God's examination. Too, God's statement was rather final: I will not overlook their sins anymore!

9. Direct members' attention to 7:10–17. As you read the text aloud, ask the class to pay attention to Amaziah's reaction to Amos and note Amos's response to Amaziah. Read the text. Then lead the class to identify Amaziah.

10. Encourage members to join with three other people seated around them for this assignment. Instruct half the groups of four to discuss Amaziah's response to Amos (7:10–13). *What was his motivation? What might have been an alternative way for him to respond to Amos?* Instruct the other groups to discuss Amos's response to Amaziah (7:14–17). *Considering Amaziah's position as priest and Amos's position as a layperson, what might have been an alternative response had Amos been less bold?*

Encourage Application

11. Pose question 3 from the *Study Guide*: *Why have Baptists historically upheld the separation of the church and the state?*

12. Ask the four debaters previously enlisted to take their positions in front of the group. Explain to the class that these members were previously selected to participate in an informal debate on this issue. Write the statement on the board; see step 1. Explain that the positions debaters take are not necessarily their own but are meant to stimulate discussion and examination of the issue. Explain to the debaters that they will have three minutes each to state their positions and their rebuttals. According to the time available after the debate, encourage discussion between the debaters and class members when the debate is over.

13. Use the small article, "Case Study," in the *Study Guide* to continue the discussion.

14. Conclude by asking for summaries of what the encounter of Amos with Amaziah suggests for our response to God today.

Teaching Plan—Lecture and Questions

Connect with Life

1. Take a plumb line or level to class with you. Begin the session by asking members to identify the tool you are holding, and its use.

2. Tell the story from step 4 of "Teaching Plan—Varied Learning Activities" about the new building's elevator shaft.

3. Explain that from today's message from Amos we will see how Israel measured up to God's plumb line.

Guide Bible Study

4. Call members' attention to Amos 7:1–9. Point out that this passage deals with three visions of Amos and involve a dialogue between the prophet and God. Ask the class to listen for each of the visions, for Amos's response, and for God's response to Amos.

5. Ask, *What was the response of Amos to God's threat in verses 8b–9?* (Amos did not respond.) Ask, *Why did Amos not respond to this third vision?* (Perhaps he knew that Israel would not measure up, or he understood the finality of God's word, "Never again.")

6. Refer the class to 7:10–15 and read it aloud. Ask the class to identify Amaziah. Be sure the class understands that Amaziah was "the court preacher," paid by King Jeroboam to deliver messages that were pleasing to the king.

7. Retell in your own words the illustration from the *Study Guide* about paid courtroom testimony. Inquire, *What similarities do you see between today's practice and Jeroboam retaining a court preacher?* (One can assume that the one being paid would likely say what the payer wanted to hear.)

8. Lead the class to speculate on the nature of Amaziah's prophecies and sermons that he delivered to the king. Ask, *What sorts of things would the king want to hear? What subjects would Amaziah NOT bring up in his sermons?* (The king's sins, including his mistreatment of the people)

9. Ask, *What do you think about the boldness of Amos in responding to Amaziah?* Before allowing for responses, immediately read aloud verses 16–17. Point out that Amos was a "mere" layman! How could he speak with such boldness? Read verse 15 aloud again. Allow for responses.

Encourage Application

10. Use the small article in the *Study Guide* about Thomas Helwys to illustrate Baptists' historical stance toward involvement of government with religion and vice versa.

11. Ask, *Could it be that Baptists' historical position on the separation of church and state is no longer valid in light of the complex moral and ethical dilemmas facing our government officials? If we lowered that wall wouldn't we be able to have more influence over our government?* Allow for ample discussion on this issue. Recall items in current news that relate to church and state, such as governmental bodies erecting religious monuments (containing, for example, the Ten Commandments). Refer to the small article, "Case Study," in the *Study Guide.*

12. Ask, *Are there ways Christians can work for justice, ways obedient to the teachings of Scripture, apart from involvement of the government? What are a Christian's responsibilities toward government?* Allow for discussion. Point out that Jesus' admonition to render to Caesar the things that are Caesar's and to God the things that are God's is an admonition to respect both.

13. Refer to comments under "God and Country" and "Implications for Today" in the *Study Guide* to summarize the lesson.

Focal Text

Amos 9

Background

Amos 9

Main Idea

God's judgment on sin is certain, as is the restoration that God offers.

Question to Explore

What can we count on God to do?

Teaching Aim

To lead the class to decide what they will do about God's message of judgment and restoration

A M O S

A God Who Roars

Lesson Five

Certain Judgment–and Hope

BIBLE COMMENTS

Understanding the Context

Amos was clearly a prophet who announced divine judgment, condemning the people of Israel for their sinful, rebellious ways, but he also saw God as forgiver and redeemer of his people. This final chapter of Amos's prophecies completes his message. God did not leave the ancient Hebrews without hope, regardless of the length or the depth of their sinfulness. Neither does God leave us without hope today.

Messages of judgment and doom are often necessary to wake up erring people to the consequences of their present deeds. To the self-confident, self-satisfied nation to which Amos spoke, strong words were needed to shake them awake to the realities of the consequences of their lives—individually and nationally. The prophets never spoke their harsh words of impending judgment because they sadistically enjoyed lashing out at the people. Throughout the Bible, God is seen as a redeeming God, always reaching out to rebellious people, always eager to forgive—if only God can find repentance. The Hebrew word for repentance means literally "to turn" or "to return." God was then, as he is now, calling for a turning around in the lives of sinful people, with a returning to him.

53

Through eight-and-a-half chapters Amos presented a dismal and fore-boding picture of divine judgment and doom for the nation. Why? To show the people how far they were from God and their need for repentance so that God could forgive them and bring them to enjoy the blessings God desired to shower on them. Chapter 9, beginning with an additional vision of judgment, soon turns to a picture of what God had in store for a people who would hear and repent, truly becoming God's people in the world.

Interpreting the Scriptures

A Vision of God Beside the Altar (9:1–4)

In this fifth and final vision reported by Amos, God was standing beside the altar. The location of this altar is unmentioned and unimportant. It may be an altar where Yahweh, their true God, was worshiped; or it may be at one of the pagan shrines, evidently common in the land.

The message told yet again is that God stands in judgment, condemning the pagan rituals and the hollow and insincere worship offered to him. His word was to strike the capitals. The capitals are the decorative section atop the columns supporting the roof of the structure. The picture Amos presents appears to be that of an earthquake. Not only would the columns collapse, even the entryway floor (the thresholds) would shake in the collapse of the building. The falling building would then collapse on the heads of the worshipers.

The vision promised that those who were left would be annihilated—"not one of them shall escape." So thorough would be the destruction that even if some could dig to Sheol or climb to heaven, they would be found and destroyed. *Sheol* is the Hebrew term for the place where the dead went and were kept. It was usually pictured as beneath the ground. It was like neither Heaven nor Hell. Rather it was a place of shadowy existence, without a positive life but neither with a total extinction of the individual. There is no good English word to translate it. *Sheol* was beyond the reach of living mortals, emphasizing the impossibility of escape.

Mount Carmel was not the highest point in Israel, but it is the highest point near the seashore. Here the appropriate contrast is the top of Carmel and the bottom of the sea. People attempting to escape the judgment of God would be found if they went to the top of Carmel. Even the sea serpent would be used by God in ferreting out those trying to escape in the sea. Even captivity, being taken away by the enemy, would not provide escape. There was no possibility of escape from the judgment of God.

A Doxology—Who Is This God Who Promises Judgment? (9:5–6)

Amos sought to make clear to his hearers and readers the greatness, might, and power of the God for whom he spoke. First, this God is the commander-in-chief of the heavenly hosts, the one who has all of the angelic host at his command. He has the power to control all of the elements of the natural world. The passage reads like a hymn of praise, emphasizing the greatness and majesty of God. At God's touch great convulsions fall on the earth. His dwelling is founded on the earth and reaches to the heavens. He gives rain to the earth. Many of Amos's contemporaries gave Baal the credit for rain and the resulting fertility on the earth. But, no: it is Yahweh who takes the waters of the sea and pours them out in rainfall on the earth.

The hymn concludes with: "Yahweh is his name" (author's translation). The name of God was important to the Hebrews. In the thought of the ancient world gods did not disclose their names to ordinary mortals. Their belief was that if you had someone's name, you had control over them, at least to a certain extent. The name was an extension of the personality of the person. Gods were known by nicknames, not their real names. The fact that God revealed his name to Moses in the wilderness was significant (Exodus 3:13–16). Israel must be a special people to possess the name of God. That is why reverence for God's name means reverence for God himself. The Hebrews had no image of their God; all they possessed was God's name. Amos said that this great God was the one coming in judgment on them.

No Claim for Special Treatment from God (9:7–10)

God was the God of the nations, even if they did not recognize him. He was in Amos's time, and he still is today. Not only had God moved the Israelites to Canaan, God was the one who moved the Philistines and the Syrians. Although God had chosen the Hebrews, they had not responded to him; they had become like the Ethiopians. Earlier Amos had affirmed God's choice of the Hebrews for a special or *elect* people (3:1–2). But in that passage as well as here, Amos clearly stated that this special relationship did not give them freedom to disobey God without suffering the consequences. In fact, their responsibility to be obedient was heightened. Along with responsibility came the certainty of judgment. His eyes were on the sinful nation for destruction. The only hope was that Israel would not be completely destroyed.

The illusion of self-confidence held by the nation is clear. They said, "Evil shall not overtake or meet us" (9:10). But God promised death to all the sinners of the people. Punishment was pictured as a *shaking* of the nation. This shaking is related to the shaking of the temple in the visions in 9:1 in that it is a message of destruction, but the shaking here is a picture of exile for the nation. The Israelites were to be exiled among the nations. The comprehensiveness of the punishment is evident in the promise that "no pebble shall fall to the ground," out of the shaking sieve (9:9).

God's punishment reaches every guilty person. Particular mention is made of the unconcerned, self-confident ones who cannot conceive of anything bad happening to them. Many of the people were like the proverbial ostrich with its head in the sand.

Hope Beyond Doom (9:11–15)

"On that day . . ." is a term frequently used by the prophets to refer to a future day of God's action, but with no specific date given. It is used to speak of God's intended action in days to come. Amos spoke of God's intention to reestablish his people. The "booth of David" is literally the shelter or temporary dwelling that is to be reestablished and made permanent in a greater and more secure time to come. A glorious age to come is pictured in graphic poetic imagery as a time of great fertility and productivity in the land. There would be a reversal of what was described earlier in 5:11, where the prophet proclaimed that the people would build houses in which they would not live and plant vineyards from which they would not enjoy the produce. Here they would rebuild cities and live in them and plant vineyards and make gardens and enjoy the produce from them. Finally they are promised security in their restored homes.

How are we to understand and interpret these verses? Israel (the Northern Kingdom, in which Amos prophesied) was conquered in 722 BC. Many of the people were exiled, never to return to the land. Foreigners moved in and intermarried with those who were left. (See 2 Kings 17:24–41.) Perhaps these verses should be applied to the other Hebrew kingdom, Judah, which was conquered and exiled in 597 and 587 BC. Some of the descendants of these Judean exiles returned to the land, not as a kingdom, but as a province beginning in 539 BC when Cyrus of Persia came to dominate the ancient world. Some interpreters have seen the fulfillment of these verses in the Jewish kingdom of the Maccabees, which flourished between 168 and 63 BC. But that was primarily a political and military kingdom rather than a religious and spiritual one. Others would relate these words to the modern state of Israel. But again, it is primarily political and military in focus rather than religious.

James, the half-brother of Jesus and leader in the early Jerusalem church, quoted a part of this passage, as reported in Acts 15:16–17, with some added statements from Jeremiah 12:15 and Isaiah 45:21. He interpreted these Scriptures to relate to the welcoming of all believers into the Christian church. The New Testament writers certainly saw the promises of the Old Testament applying to and being fulfilled in their day. The New Testament does indeed complete and fulfill the Old Testament. The believers in Christ become the Israel of faith and the inheritors of God's promises.

The whole question of promise and fulfillment requires another consideration. God's promises to Israel were conditional. Look back to the establishment of the covenant nation as reported in Exodus 19:5–6. The nation was gathered at the foot of Mount Sinai where Moses reported to them the words of Yahweh: " . . . If you obey my voice and keep my covenant . . . you shall be for me a priestly kingdom and a holy nation." The "if" was a regular part of God's promises to his people. God's election or choice of a people was not just to a privileged position but was primarily to service for him. He could and did, as Paul put it, break off branches from the covenant nation and graft in branches, the Christian Gentiles, into his covenant people (Romans 11:17–20). We also must remember that God is not finished with the world yet. The future is still in God's hands.

Focusing on the Meaning

God condemns sin and sinful people, individuals and nations. From God's righteous judgment there is no escape. Israel was going along in smug self-satisfaction, feeling that they, in the prosperous kingdom ruled by Jeroboam II, were in control of their own destiny. Similar attitudes are prevalent in our day. The patience of God in delaying the deserved punishment of God's people was seen by the average Israelite as proof that God was either unconcerned or unable to do anything. Many in the twenty-first century have similar thoughts—or even deny that a God exists. God's judgment, though, is both certain and absolutely inescapable.

We need to have a clearer picture of this God we serve and worship. Amos pictured God in ways that were meaningful for his generation. We might add to his description some modern pictures. I marvel at the capability of this computer on which I am writing this lesson. It tells me whenever I misspell a word, and in a second or less it can tell me how many words I have written on this lesson. It remembers what I wrote years ago. It can put me in touch with relatives and friends across the world almost in a flash. But the great God we serve knows all my words and all my thoughts—past, present, and future.

God understands the ways of all the great sea creatures I have never seen. He sent the thunderstorm that awoke me last night and the rain to water the parched ground. Our words cannot "touch the hem of his garment"—such is God's greatness, power, and majesty. Yet God knows my name and permits me to know his name and call on him. To top it all, God loves me and poured himself out in the person of his Son to die on a cross for my sins. This is the God we are called on to accept and serve.

Even in the midst of a sinful world, filled with injustice, oppression, and all manner of evil, a forgiving and loving God was and still is seeking to redeem his rebelling creation. The marvel of our Scriptures is that God would have such love and concern for people like ancient Israel and like us. The prophets in chorus proclaim that with God there is not only a future, but there is also hope in that future.

We may struggle with exactly how to understand the future referred to by Amos (and other prophets as well). After spending more than forty years studying and teaching these prophets, I still struggle, too. But this I know, the future is in God's hands, and my primary response must be to trust God. He is totally capable. He will do what is right and good. If all would love and serve God, all of the good that God desires for us would come to pass.

TEACHING PLANS

Teaching Plan—Varied Learning Activities

Connect with Life

1. *Prior to the session:* Get pencils and a pack of 3 x 5 index cards. Enlist four volunteers to participate in the monologue at the end of this teaching plan. Ask them to rehearse their lines so they can express them with feeling (although memorization is unnecessary).

2. Begin the session by pointing out that the first six chapters of Amos contain the "words of Amos" as delivered by God's spokesman. The last three chapters contain Amos's five visions. In this last vision recorded in chapter 9, Amos was silent as he listened to God's voice. It is though God had gotten so fed up with Israel's sin that he would no longer use a spokesman. Instead God addressed Israel directly and forcefully.

Guide Bible Study

3. Encourage the class to turn to Amos 9. Use this illustration: Ask who remembers the Washington-area sniper saga from October, 2002. In the midst of the frantic search for the snipers, CNN reported on the various tools the police had at their disposal, including satellite photography. Starting with a view of the earth from hundreds of miles in outer space showing only a vague outline of the continent, the camera gradually zoomed in. Features began to take shape, such as cleared and forested areas, then developed areas, then streams and streets. Finally, into view came a very clear shot of the basketball court near the crime scene! Can even this fantastic capability begin to compare with God's ability to see into the recesses of our personal hideaways, even our own hearts?

4. As you (or a good reader whom you enlist) read 9:1–4 aloud, ask the class to listen to places where Israel might be able to hide from God. After reading, ask for responses (there are no hiding places!).

5. Point out that verses 5–8a remind us of why there is no place to hide. Read these verses, and then ask: *Why is there no place to hide from God?* (He is the all-powerful, Creator God!).

6. Ask, *Can you recall why God was so angry with Israel? What specific sins so offended God?* As needed point out Israel's treatment of the poor.

7. Cue the four volunteers to read their monologues.

Monologues

Person 1 (Israel): (boastfully) We're God's chosen people!

Person 2: How do you like my new shoes? I got them with the extra profit I made. What's wrong with charging what the traffic will bear?

Person 1: God loved us so much God brought us out of Egypt and gave us this beautiful land!

Person 3: (sarcastically) Sure I threw them out on the street! I can't help that he lost his job—they weren't paying their rent!

Person 1: We strictly abide by God's laws! Why, we even go beyond them, making them even stricter! We are *very* religious.

Person 4: (plaintively) Oh, I know we didn't need the room, but if we hadn't traded up to get that tax break we'd have lost all that money!

---

8. Point the class's attention to verses 8b–15. As you (or a volunteer) read these verses aloud, ask the class to note the surprise that is found here, in light of God's stern judgment just voiced. After the reading, call for response about the surprise (God was offering hope even in the midst of severe judgment).

9. Use question 3 from the *Study Guide*, or rephrase the question like this: *Why would God offer such hope when he was so angry with Israel?*

Encourage Application

10. Put this statement from the *Study Guide* on the board: "We cannot look at past experiences and ignore present realities. Living for Christ is not a one-time salvation experience that means we can live as we please beyond our baptism." Ask: *What does this statement say to you?*

11. Instruct class members to move their chairs together with three other people (two others if the class is small) and discuss question 2 from the *Study Guide*. Allow five to seven minutes for discussion, and then invite volunteers to share their answers.

12. Ask these same groups to read and discuss the case study from the *Study Guide.*

13. Close with guided prayer. Lead class members to bow their heads and pray silently as you guide them as follows: *First, ask God's forgiveness for a specific sin that pervades American culture. Next, thank God for God's patience with us, and for the promise of God's forgiveness and grace. Finally, ask God to reveal to you something specific you can do to be God's instrument of grace where you live and work.*

Teaching Plan—Lecture and Questions

Connect with Life

1. Prior to the session, research the following information from your church office or church clerk:

   • Find baptism statistics for your church for the past year. If available secure the data for the past five years.
   • Research the number of specific ministries of your church to the poor.
   • Calculate the percentage of building indebtedness to the total church budget.
   • Calculate the amount of the budget that is spent primarily on the church's membership and how much is specifically for those beyond the church.

2. On the board, write this outline:

> Amos 1—6 God's message through Amos
> Amos 7—8 Amos's visions of God's actions
> Amos 9 Amos's vision of God's proclamation

Guide Bible Study

3. Make Bible-searching assignments as follows: Ask half the class to work as individuals to review 7:1–9; 8:1–3 for the subject of four of Amos's visions. Ask the other half of the class to scan Amos 1—6 as individuals to identify the sins of Israel that had so angered God. After about five minutes, receive reports. For the first assignment, write the vision on the left half of the board as it is identified. For the second assignment, write the sins on the right half of the board.

4. Point out that in the last vision, in chapter 9, Amos was silent as he listened to God speak for himself in judgment of Israel.

5. Ask the class to listen as you read 9:1–4 for what God assumed Israel was going to try to do as he implemented judgment (hide, escape, or run). Ask, *Would Israel succeed in their effort to escape God's judgment? Why not?*

6. Ask members to turn to Romans 8:38–39 and read silently. Ask, *How is Romans 8:38–39 different from Amos 9:1–4?* (Amos 9:1–4 says there is no escaping God's judgment. Rom. 8:38–39 says there is no escaping God's love). Ask, *How can we reconcile the meaning of these passages?* (See the *Study Guide* comments.) Ask, *Who will receive the wrath of God?* (those who are not in Christ, who are not obedient to God)

7. Ask, *What is the purpose of Amos 9:5–7?* (To show the greatness of God) Point out that Israel seemed to assume that their special status as God's "chosen" gave them immunity to God's judgment. Ask, *How do we presume on God's patience?*

8. Explain that although God offers hope in 9:8–15, only a remnant would receive God's promised grace.

9. Lead the class to recall the reason God sent the prophets to Israel: to remind them of *why* they had special status before God. Point out that God blessed Israel for a purpose: that they might become

God's instruments of reconciliation and grace in the world. When they ultimately failed to get the point and to heed God's warnings, God put into place a new plan, the church, who would be charged with carrying out his plan.

Encourage Application

10. Guide the class to turn to 2 Corinthians 5:17–20. Enlist a member who reads well to read this passage aloud. Invite the class to listen for these things: *Who began the work of reconciliation? To whom is the ministry of reconciliation given? What is the place of the church (and its individual members) according to this passage?* Allow for responses to each of these questions.

11. Ask, *How would God evaluate (judge) the efforts of our church with regard to 2 Corinthians 5:18–20?* After some discussion, cite the statistics you researched as mentioned in step 1.

12. Refer to and read this comment from the *Study Guide* in the last paragraph under "Certain Judgment (9:1–8a)": "We cannot look at past experiences and ignore present realities. Living for Christ is not a one-time salvation experience that means we can live as we please beyond our baptism." Pose question 2 from the *Study Guide* concerning Baptists' presumption on our salvation experiences. Allow for responses. Then ask, *How might we be presuming on God's patience?*

13. Close with prayer that God will make the prophecy of Amos real to us, as God's remnant, charged with the ministry of reconciling the lost to God and reconciling estranged people to one another. Pray for forgiveness for the times we have played at being church, for when we have spent more on ourselves than we have to reach a lost world. Pray for the Spirit's leadership in becoming effective ambassadors for Christ.

Main Idea

Unfaithfulness to God leads to rejection by God.

Question to Explore

Does God really punish sin?

Teaching Aim

To lead the class to summarize how Hosea's family relationships conveyed God's message of judgment to Israel and state implications for life today

HOSEA

A God Who Judges and Restores

Lesson Six

Trouble in the Family

BIBLE COMMENTS

Understanding the Context

Many times, the truth hurts. The Book of Hosea reminds us that even the truth God wants to teach us can be painful. In order to learn these truths and convey them to his fellow countrymen, the prophet had to endure a broken heart and a broken marriage. Yet, in spite of the hurt, Hosea learned of God's love, grace, and forgiveness through a series of personal illustrations he would never forget. These truths would form the basis of Hosea's message to Israel.

This first book among the minor prophets is the story of a man's love for his adulterous wife and God's love for his chosen, yet sinful, people. This book is also the story of God's people and how low they had sunk morally and spiritually. To appreciate the depth of God's love, one must consider the depths of Israel's sin.

Hosea lived in Israel, the Northern Kingdom, during the last half of the eighth century BC. More than likely he began his ministry during the reign of King Jeroboam II and continued for many years after Jeroboam's death in 748 BC. Hosea was a contemporary of Isaiah and Amos. It is probable that Hosea's ministry continued until after Israel fell to the Assyrians in 722 BC. Perhaps Hosea finished his career in the Southern Kingdom of Judah. What an incredible testimony he would have for the Southern Kingdom as an eyewitness to the judgment of God on the Northern Kingdom.

Hosea's audience suffered from a theological and political crisis. The worship of the Canaanite fertility god Baal is mentioned specifically several times in the book (see 2:8, 13, 17; 11:2; 13:1). Baal worship included ritual prostitution to ensure timely rains and abundant crops. Likewise, the political climate was very unstable as Israel's kings became puppets to the Assyrian Empire. Following Jeroboam II, six kings ruled within a period of twenty years. Several of them were assassinated, and the turmoil surrounding the throne took its toll on the nation. An interesting thing happened economically during this period. The rich got richer and the poor got poorer. The middle class all but disappeared. This led to many of the social injustices that Hosea spoke against.

To help the prophet understand the seriousness of the nation's sin, God instructed him to take an adulterous wife and to name their children with names that reflected God's displeasure with God's people. This most unusual request certainly affected Hosea's career, his marriage, and the lives of his children. As people would ask about his children's unusual names, Hosea would have the opportunity to explain how God had rejected Israel for their sins. Of course, his marriage and commitment to a prostitute would also provide a good illustration of God's grace.

Interpreting the Scriptures

It's All About the "Word" (1:1)

1:1. The Book of Hosea is our only source of information about the prophet. His name occurs four times in the book, all in the first chapter. It means *deliverance, rescue, salvation,* or *safety.* It is very close to the name Joshua (*the Lord saves*) and the name Jesus. It is the same word as Hoshea (last king of Israel) but is always rendered with *s* instead of *sh* in order to avoid confusion between the two. Hosea's name seems fitting in that his family and his nation needed deliverance. It is also interesting that Hosea and Jesus share the same Hebrew name given that they both suffered personally in order to convey the truth.

Because of several references to the priesthood (4:6–8; 5:1; 6:9), some have suggested that Hosea was a priest. Indeed, he makes references to the law and to things clean and unclean (8:12; 9:3). Others suggest he was a farmer because of several illustrations from agricultural life. Still others think he was a baker based on his illustration in 7:4–8. What we know is that Hosea was an obedient follower of Yahweh who was very familiar with the spiritual condition of his fellow Jews.

Using his dysfunctional family as a living illustration and preaching such a harsh message was not Hosea's idea. It came straight from God. It was a word applicable to the people living then as well as to people living today. Regardless of the different interpretations of this unusual command about marrying a prostitute, the truth that the story conveys is from God.

Although Hosea's message was primarily to the Northern Kingdom of Israel, four of the Southern Kingdom's monarchs are listed. The combined reigns of Uzziah, Jotham, Ahaz, and Hezekiah total 113 years. However, if we consider Hosea's career to begin during the last year of Uzziah and continue through the sixth year of Hezekiah (722 BC), then we have a more plausible span of 40 years. Mentioning the Judean kings would identify Hosea as a contemporary of Isaiah (see Isaiah 1:1).

Although Hosea's ministry lasted through seven Israelite kings, only one is mentioned. Jeroboam the son of Joash is referred to as Jeroboam II to distinguish him from the Northern Kingdom's first king, Jeroboam the son of Nebat.

It's All About Obedience (1:2–3)

1:2. The opening phrase seems to indicate the beginning of Hosea's prophetic career. There is a difference of opinion, however, about God's initial instructions. Those who choose the allegorical interpretation argue that the marriage to Gomer was not an historical event. They can not understand God telling this man to marry a prostitute. However, other Bible scholars today take the command literally. Gomer was a real person who either was a prostitute before marrying Hosea or turned to that lifestyle after the marriage. The name *Gomer* has no symbolic meaning, as one might expect if the story was allegorical.

The phrase "adulterous wife" is the translation of the plural form of the word *harlotry*. The plural intensifies the definition and reflects a pattern or lifestyle of repeated sexual sin. This makes Gomer an even more fitting symbol of Israel, since the nation had repeatedly been unfaithful to Yahweh. God commanded Hosea to enter into such a relationship so that the prophet could understand God's point of view with Israel. The purpose of the marriage was so that Hosea, with his broken heart over such a wife, could see how the sins of his people had repeatedly broken the heart of God. Obviously, Hosea's first-hand experiences would help him communicate this truth to God's people.

Hosea's call in this verse also mentions the "children of unfaithfulness." The reputation of their mother would precede the children and affect their lives, just as the reputation of the unfaithfulness of previous generations affected the contemporaries of Hosea. People's sins can affect future generations.

1:3. Hosea's obedience to this very unusual request speaks volumes about his character and faithfulness. There is no indication that the prophet argued with God or worried about his reputation. In fact, if Hosea was a priest and Gomer was already a prostitute, then the marriage would have violated the Mosaic law. Certainly Hosea had plenty of grounds to contest this divine request. However, he simply obeyed.

The identification of Gomer as "daughter of Diblaim" reinforces the idea that Gomer was a real person and that her marriage to Hosea was an historical event. Soon they had a son.

It's All About the Names (1:4–9)

1:4–5. God instructed Hosea to name the firstborn son Jezreel. The word means *God sows.* Jezreel was the name of a very fertile valley that separated the regions of Galilee and Samaria. The name suggests that God personally planted the lush vegetation. For Hosea, however, the name referred to the massacre of the house of Ahab approximately eighty years prior. Although Jehu had been told by God to destroy the house of King Ahab (2 Kings 9:7), Jehu's slaughter went far beyond God's intention. At Jezreel, Jehu displayed seventy heads of Ahab's princes (2 Kings 10:1–11). Jehu also killed forty-two visiting relatives of Ahaziah, King of Judah (2 Kings 10:12–14).

By naming his son Jezreel, Hosea was prophesying that the Northern Kingdom of Israel would come to an end, just as Ahab's dynasty came to an end in that particular valley. There is a play on words between Jezreel and Israel. They look and sound very similar in Hebrew. It is ironic that in such a fertile valley God would bring death and destruction.

The reference to breaking "Israel's bow" was a prediction of military defeat. By 733 BC, Tiglath-Pileser III of Assyria began to raid and take captives from the valley area. A few years later, the entire Northern Kingdom would lie in ruins. God's people were warned repeatedly of the impending judgment. One such warning was the son of a prophet and prostitute named Jezreel walking around town.

1:6–7. The second child, a girl, was to be named Lo-Ruhamah. The name means *not loved* or *no compassion*. Having a name like this would certainly affect a woman's self-esteem and overall quality of life. God's message to his people that he would no longer have compassion was certainly meant to affect how the community of disbelief felt about themselves and their sin. God was announcing that he would no longer forgive Israel for their sins.

The tragic lesson here is that a group of people who repeatedly engage in sin and rebellion can reach a point beyond grace and forgiveness. Judgment was the only recourse God had left. This verse suggests that the covenant bond between Yahweh and his people has been broken. Their unfaithfulness and spiritual adultery by turning to other gods had finally taken its toll. God would use the Assyrian Empire to bring justice to his people.

However, there is a sense of grace and compassion in verse 7 as God announced that he would continue to love the Southern Kingdom, Judah. Several periods of revival and reform, led by godly kings, had kept Judah from sliding as far away as their brothers to the North. Although certainly not perfect, they would receive God's grace. Their salvation would come not from their military might; rather, it would come from God. Indeed, God intervened and delivered Judah from the Assyrians in 701 BC (see 2 Kings 19).

1:8–9. The third child born (two or three years later, "after she had weaned Lo-Ruhamah") was named Lo-Ammi, a name that means *not my people*. If there is any doubt that God's people had broken the covenant, this third name settles the issue. God's relationship with his people had always been expressed in the phrase, "You are my people" (see Exodus 6:7; Leviticus 26:12; Deuteronomy 26:18). Israel's idolatry broke that covenant. While the child's name may also reflect the possibility that he was not the biological child of Hosea, its broader meaning for the nation is unmistakable.

These three children, and the names they would carry all of their lives, were sermon illustrations that would keep on preaching for years to come. As God so often does, God had communicated his truth in a relevant manner that certainly attracted attention. While this message of judgment was obviously not pleasant for the messenger, its meaning for the intended recipients was devastating.

Focusing on the Meaning

As God's people living under the new covenant, we tend to emphasize God's grace. Indeed, that is what the gospel is all about. However, we must remember that the Bible also teaches that God punishes sin. Grace is not a doormat that we can flagrantly wipe our sinful feet on again and again. Unfaithfulness to God leads to rejection by God. He is a God of wrath and judgment.

Hosea's imagery of marriage is one with which many can identify. Perhaps someone in your Bible study group can identify with the hurt and pain of having an unfaithful spouse. Many times, we offer forgiveness and another chance. However, repeated instances of infidelity often offer only one solution. The relationship must be terminated. As tragic as that common scenario is, it does provide us with a glimpse of how God must feel when we abandon him to chase other gods.

As serious as adultery is, so is spiritual adultery. Many Christians today are guilty of cheating on God. Although we do not think of idolatry as a particular problem in twenty-first century America, we do worship many different things. Our lives are full of things that can easily be placed on a higher pedestal than God. The truth from Hosea is that God will not tolerate that kind of behavior.

The problem with reconciling God's mercy and judgment is our view of justice. We tend to think of judgment as vindication or retribution, as "getting even." However, God uses judgment in a redemptive way. His treatment of the Northern Kingdom helped Judah (and us today!) understand the seriousness of sin. Similarly, God's judgment on others provides lessons for all of us.

In what ways has the punishment of sin affected your life directly and indirectly? What lessons can be learned from these instances? Do these events in our lives provide an opportunity to explain to a non-believer the love of God?

TEACHING PLANS

Teaching Plan—Varied Learning Activities

Connect with Life

1. Prior to class, cut a live flower with many petals from your garden, or purchase an inexpensive one. As the class session begins, start pulling the petals off one at a time and say, "He loves me," after the first one, "He loves me not," after the next one, and continue alternating these until all petals are pulled off. Note that in our study today we are going to see the actions of real love even in the time of judgment.

2. Before the class time, prepare two tear sheets, one with the word *Amos* written across the top, and the other with the word *Hosea*. Leave enough room for writing information below the words. Divide the class in half and ask them to work in twos or threes to complete these assignments: One half is to describe the approach Amos used in presenting his message to the people, and the second half is to describe the approach of Hosea. Information for completing each assignment can be found in the *Study Guide* under "Background of the Biblical Story." Call for answers and select a person to write them on the tear sheets.

3. Ask members to again work in twos and threes to discuss which approach, Hosea's or Amos's, is the most appealing to them, and why. Then have groups share their answers with the class.

4. In advance assign a class member the responsibility of giving a brief lecture on the national life during Hosea's time from the *Study Guide*. Call for this report now.

Guide Bible Study

5. Ask these questions:
   * What major commitments have you made in your life?
   * Did anyone command you to make that commitment?

Have a member read Hosea 1:1–2 aloud. Ask the class to listen for the answers to these questions:

- What commitment was Hosea asked to make?
- Who commanded him to make this commitment?

6. Call for responses and then ask: *Why do you think God told Hosea to do this?* (Note that Hosea obeyed God's command.) Have members share what their reaction would be if God asked them to do this.

7. Point out that in our study today we will discover that there is more involved than a marriage relationship. Ask, *Whom did Hosea represent, and whom did Gomer represent?* (God, Israel) Explain as needed.

8. Form three study groups. Have each group select their leader. Ask them to research the following information you have written on an instruction sheet. Assign each group a different child's name from Hosea 1:4–9. Instruct each group to report on the meaning of the child's name and what God would do in his relationship with his people. After a few minutes, have them report to the group. They can find information in their *Study Guides*. (If the class is small, a group could be just one or two people working together.) After about five minutes, call for reports.

9. Select one of the members to record answers on the board as the members respond to the following comment: *Describe the feelings you think would be present in a person if someone was unfaithful to him or her.* After they have completed their list, ask: *How does this list assist you in understanding how God feels toward those who are unfaithful to him?*

Encourage Application

10. Ask question 5 and then question 6 from the *Study Guide*.

11. Have a member read aloud the small article, "Spirituality," from the *Study Guide*. Call for responses to the question at the end of the article, and then use these questions to continue discussion:

- How does our church compare to this church we have just read about?
- Do we need to make any changes in our church?

12. Invite volunteers to summarize the implications of the lesson for life today. Refer to the Main Idea as needed.

Teaching Plan—Lecture and Questions

Connect with Life

1. Before class write the title of the lesson on the board or a poster. To begin the class session, use the story about Emily in the *Study Guide*, or write one of your own. Ask the two questions at the close of the story about Emily.

2. State that Hosea's story is the story of a troubled family. Refer to the lesson title. Remark that the story is also about God's relationship with God's troubled family.

Guide Bible Study

3. Using the material found under the heading "Background of the Biblical Story" in the *Study Guide*, lecture briefly to help the members understand the times in which Hosea lived.

4. Refer to the first outline point, "Yahweh's Word (1:1)." Point out that the Lord, not Hosea, is the main character of this book and is directing the events. Ask these questions:

   • How well do we listen for a word from God?
   • How does God speak to us today?

5. Refer to the second outline point, "When Yahweh's Word Intersects Human Living (1:2)." Ask: *What would make Hosea marry a prostitute?* Then ask a member to read verse 2 so that we can discover the answer.

6. Comment that Gomer represents Israel, and Hosea, Yahweh. Ask: *Why do you think God would choose Hosea to represent him in this drama that is unfolding?* (Evidently he was faithful to God and was listening.) *How does God choose people to do his work today?* (Because they listen.) *What are some ways Hosea could have reacted to God's directions to him?* Note that Hosea was courageous in his obedience.

7. Compare the relationship of Hosea and Gomer with the relationship God had with Israel. Point out that the commandments given to Moses were still to be obeyed, and yet Israel was worshiping many gods.

8. Refer to the third outline point, "When People Become More Than Living Symbols (1:2–9)." State that Hosea's children's names came as a result of God's naming each child. Tell the story found in the *Study Guide* about the mother describing her children.

9. Make three flash cards and write the name of each child on a separate card. Tape the first child's name on the wall. Have a class member read verses 3–5 about the first child. Have the class listen for

   • The meaning of the name
   • The judgment against Israel for her unfaithfulness to Yahweh that was implied in this name

   (For more historical background about the meaning of the name of the first child, read 2 Kings 9—10.)

10. Do the same for the next two children. The second child is discussed in verses 6–7. The third child is discussed in verses 8–9.

Encourage Application

11. Refer to the fourth outline point, "Implications for Today." Guide discussion by using the following questions:

    • How do you think God would compare the situation in our day with the situation in Hosea's day?
    • To what extent do you think the church is allowing allegiance to the false gods of the world to hinder its worship of the one true God?

Focal Text

Hosea 1:10—2:5,
14–23; 3:1–5

Background

Hosea 1:10—3:5

Main Idea

God takes action to
restore people who have
gone away from him.

Question to
Explore

How does God respond to
us when we have sinned?

Teaching Aim

To help the class draw
implications for how God
wishes to relate to us from
what the passage teaches
about the relationship
God desired with Israel

HOSEA

A God Who Judges
and Restores

Lesson Seven

Restoring the Relationship

BIBLE COMMENTS

Understanding the Context

The truth that God punishes sin is not an easy
truth to deal with, and the personal applications
are hard to accept. God is also gracious and
compassionate. The message of Hosea emphasizes both of these characteristics of God.
Again, the prophet's relationship with his wife
serves as an illustration of God's relationship
with God's people.

The shift in tone at the conclusion of chapter
1, a shift from judgment to hope, is a shift that
happens repeatedly in the Book of Hosea. The
two different themes alternate throughout the
book as a reminder of the complexity of God's
character. Just as the naming of Hosea's children
illustrates the message of judgment, so the
renaming of the children in Hosea 2:1 illustrates
the message of mercy.

The second chapter, written in poetic form, is
very complex. There are at least three different
levels on which one can find meaning. The first
is the question of whether this section is about
Hosea and Gomer or God and God's people.
The second level to deal with is the apparent
tension between the righteousness of God that
demands obedience and the mercy of God that

74

allows another chance. A third level to interpret is the image of God as a husband. Although not as common as the theme of God as Father, it is an appropriate image for Hosea to use.

The third chapter presents an opportunity for more interpretation. The question that naturally arises is whether the event in Hosea 3 is the same as in Hosea 1. If it is not, then chapter 3 deals with Gomer leaving her family after the birth of her children. If it is the same event, then chapter 3 is another account of how Hosea married Gomer. A third argument, however, is that the two chapters refer to two different women.

Hosea 3 is similar to the first in that God issued a command, the prophet obeyed, and then the theological implications for Israel are explained. As you study, consider the implications and applications for life in the twenty-first century.

Interpreting the Scriptures

The Charges (1:10–2:5)

1:10. The language in this verse reminds one of the promises God made to Abraham regarding the population explosion of his descendants (see Genesis 22:17). The reiteration of this promise was an encouragement to a nation facing a hostile takeover by the Assyrians. However, more than just increasing numbers is involved in this promise; Israel would grow spiritually as well. God would bless them numerically as they returned to the covenant. Those who had been called "not my people" (as demonstrated by the name of Hosea's second son and third child) would be again called "sons of the living God." Evidence of this transition would be seen in the growing population.

1:11. "The people of Judah" were those in the Southern Kingdom while the people of Israel were those in the North. Divided after the reign of Solomon, it was the dream of many that the two nations would one day be reunited. This reuniting would be seen as the ultimate blessing from God. While the previous verse builds on a patriarchal theme (the promise to Abraham), this verse builds on a Davidic theme, namely, the glory and prosperity known by the twelve tribes while united under one monarchy. The phrase "come up out of the land" is reminiscent of the Exodus of the twelve tribes from Egypt. Again, images from the Jews' history play an important role in describing their future.

The phrase, "day of Jezreel," may refer to the incidents mentioned in the commentary on 1:4 (see lesson one). Indeed, in many ways, those events signaled the beginning of the end of Israel. The same people who were humiliated in Jezreel would one day become numerous and great. The reference may also be to the fertility of the valley, an appropriate image to the reunified, prosperous kingdom. However, some interpret the reference as to the Messianic time. Since the word "Jezreel" means *God sows*, it may allude to a future time when God would sow the seeds of redemption through the work of the Messiah. Indeed, if the promises of this passage are to be taken as a reference to the New Testament church, this interpretation seems best.

2:1. The concluding verse of this section, this instruction seems as if it must have been given to the firstborn son, Jezreel. His name originally referred to judgment, and now in light of the previous verse refers to mercy. Part of that mercy gives him the right to change the names of his brother and sister. The renaming of Hosea's children bears further witness to the grace of God.

Was this prophecy ever fulfilled? The people of the Northern Kingdom were encouraged by their Assyrian captors to marry other ethnic groups and thus dilute the pure Jewish blood line. The descendants of these mixed marriages would later become the Samaritans of the New Testament. Thus, the literal fulfillment of these verses seems impossible. The Northern Kingdom itself was not restored. Although some say that a future eschatological event will include the twelve Jewish tribes, others state that the fulfillment comes in the church. Thus the blessings intended for Judah and Israel have been given to all of those who profess the name of Jesus as the Messiah, Lord, and Savior.

2:2–5. These verses describe a scene from a legal proceeding in which a betrayed Hosea called on his children to bring a case against their adulterous mother. The word translated "rebuke" in the New International Version is translated "plead" in the King James Version. The New English Bible reads "plead my cause." Just as God asked Hosea to help convict his people of their sin, the prophet was asking the children to help convince their mother that her lifestyle was wrong. The charges brought against Gomer are the same as the charges brought against Israel. In this scene, the husband is Yahweh, the unfaithful wife is Israel, and the children are the individual Israelites who might be hearing or reading Hosea's words. The lovers would be the Baals to which Israel had turned.

The "adulterous look on her face" could have referred to some sort of identification on her face worn by prostitutes at that time. The "unfaithfulness from between her breasts" could have referred to the jewelry she might wear. The threat of nakedness in verse 3 would be the ultimate humiliation. The talk of a "desert" and "thirst" could be a way of saying the husband would completely abandon his wife, not even caring for her most basic needs.

The Covenant (2:14-23)

2:14–15. After pronouncements of two judgments against Israel in 2:6–8 and 2:9–13, the lawsuit takes an unusual twist as the language of the second half of the chapter changes from judgment to courtship. God promised to once again seek out Israel as a suitor would court his bride. The references to the Exodus (desert, Egypt) are unmistakable. The "Valley of Achor" refers to the place where Achan buried what he had taken from Jericho (Joshua 7:16–26). The name of the valley literally means "trouble." Having their "troubles" turn to hope would cause a positive response. In fact, the word "sing" could also be translated "respond" (NRSV).

2:16–17. The phrase "in that day" of verses 16, 18, and 21 sounds like an eschatological reference indicating that the fulfillment of this verse refers to a particular period of time. The courtship would begin when Israel was willing to relate to God once again as a bride relates to her husband. The word translated "my master" is a form of the word Baal. Perhaps God's people had become so distorted in their worshiping the Canaanite fertility god Baal that they confused him with Yahweh. Even today, some people say that the God of Christianity is the same God of other religions simply known by different names.

2:18–20. These verses reflect the biblical theme that a future blessing would benefit the animal kingdom as well as humankind and thus a sense of safety and security would extend to all of God's creation. The word "betroth" in verses 19 and 20 refers to a relationship that would ultimately result in marriage. This union between God and his people would last forever. A rich vocabulary is used to describe that relationship. Righteousness, justice, love, compassion, and faithfulness certainly refer to the way God relates to us today through Jesus Christ.

2:21–23. This new day of a new covenant is also depicted as a day of agricultural blessings. The day would be characterized by plenty of grain, wine, and oil. Once again, there is a reference to the valley with a name that means *God sows*—"Jezreel"—as an indication of abundance. The spiritual blessings of that day are emphasized by the reversal of the names of the prophet's children. The ones who were "not loved" would now be loved and those considered "not my people" would be "my people." The people would consequently respond to God by acknowledging him as such.

The Compassion (3:1–5)

There are three different major interpretations of the events described in chapter 3 and how it relates to chapter 1. (1) One interpretation is that the events in chapter 3 record what happened after Gomer abandoned her family and had to be "bought" back by Hosea. Perhaps she had returned to a life of adultery and become enslaved to another man. (2) Another interpretation is that the events in chapters 1 and 3 are the same, told from different perspectives. (3) A third major interpretation is that chapter 3 is about a different woman altogether. Since Gomer is never named in chapter 3, this argument says that Hosea was being instructed to marry another prostitute to make the same point again. The first interpretation makes the most sense to this writer.

3:1. In the NIV, a form of the word "love" is used five times. These five uses refer to four different types of love, with two of the uses having a similar meaning. The instruction for Hosea to love his wife speaks of the kind of love that only a husband and wife can experience. Indeed, this kind of love is a gift from God. The second use of the word describes the wife's relationship to a man who was not her husband. This kind of love knows nothing of commitment or honesty. The third use of the word "love" refers to the love God has for his people by using the illustration of Hosea's love for Gomer. Like the first love, this kind is true and wholesome. The fourth love mentioned is the people's love for the raisin-cakes used in an annual festival to Baal. This is a misdirected love that, like the second type, is based on deceit and temporary pleasures.

3:2–3. The fact that the prophet had to use money and goods to purchase Gomer may indicate that he had a problem raising enough cash. He had to make a sacrifice to obtain her. According to some calculations, this combination would equal thirty shekels, the cost of a slave. Just as

Hosea had to pay a high price to demonstrate his love for Gomer, so Christ had to pay for our sins because of his love for us.

Hosea has some restrictions for Gomer. She was to live with him and cease her sinful activities. The phrase "many days" is emphatic in the Hebrew. She would have to practice discipline and self-control. The word translated "live with" can also mean *wait* and may indicate a period of time before Hosea would be intimate again with his wife. Only time could cure her old infatuations. The same is true with God's idolatrous people. In the case of the Southern Kingdom, seventy years of living in exile were required to finally cure them of worshiping idols.

3:4–5. Kings represented political independence. Sacred stones were used in the worship of Baal. The ephod was used by the high priest to help determine future events. All of these represented security. The people would have to learn to live without these things they had become so familiar with and dependent on. Just as Gomer would have to abstain from her fleshly desires, so would God's people. Although we have no idea how long a time period exists between verse 4 and verse 5, the central truth is that there is an "afterward," a time in which the spiritual exile is over and the people enjoy fellowship with God. The reference to King David may indeed be a Messianic reference, as Jesus Christ became the ultimate fulfillment of this promise.

Focusing on the Meaning

The message of hope and compassion, intertwined with the message of judgment, gives us good reason to always trust in God. Even in the midst of God's wrath, there are blessings to wait for and lessons to learn. The various allusions to Israel's past and how good God had been to them gave them a basis for believing God's promises about the future. The same is true in our lives today. By remembering the blessings of yesterday, we believe in the blessings of tomorrow.

Many of the promises made by God were fulfilled in the New Testament church, the spiritual Israel. God's chosen people, particularly the Northern Kingdom, could no longer be used by God. Sometimes we are tempted to think that God needs us so much to do something that no one else can do. We might think that a certain group or denomination or church is indispensable, and thus become complacent. Just as God transferred blessings originally offered to the Jews to all Gentile believers (Romans 11:17–24), so God can use anyone to do what he has called us to do.

God's plea for Israel to abandon their idols is the same plea heard many times today as God repeatedly asks us to forsake the things we place before him. While it may not be physical statues of fictitious deities that you worship, it may well be physical things. Our materialistic society has made gods out of so many things that we desire and say that we cannot live without.

Perhaps you know someone who is guilty of sexual sin like Gomer. Many times, people feel that such sins are beyond God's mercy. How can you relay the truth that God continues to love them and waits for their repentance? Can you explain the truths of the Book of Hosea in such a way as to convey this important truth?

Hosea's reconciliation with his wife is a story of a unique love and commitment that is hard to find today. Many troubled marriages are ended because of the lack of effort to save the relationship. Neither party is willing to make the sacrifice. Hosea went far beyond the second mile to restore his marriage. Would you be willing to go to such lengths to save your marriage?

TEACHING PLANS

Teaching Plan—Varied Learning Activities

Connect with Life

1. On the board (or a poster), write the Question to Explore. Have it on the wall as the members enter the room.

2. Ask this question: *Have you ever had to buy back something that was once yours?* Share a personal experience; ask a class member to be ready to share a personal experience, or tell the following story:

    Mary made a beautiful quilt that had special remembrances from their children's early years. They used it on their bed for many years. One day it was stolen from their home. Six months later, as Mary and her husband were walking through a flea market, they spotted their quilt. Because the operator of the booth had bought the quilt to sell, Mary had to buy it back. She said, "I made you once, and bought you back; you are now twice mine."

3. Point out that in today's lesson we are going to discover that God told Hosea to go and bring Gomer back the second time. God is in the business of restoring relationships. As we study, we will find the answer to the question that is written on the board (or poster).

Guide Bible Study

4. Have a member that you have enlisted before class to read Hosea 1:10—2:1 aloud. Ask the class to listen for indications that God was going to restore the relationship.

5. Select a member to record the answers on the board as the class reports. (Example: Lo-Ruhamah meant "not my people" and is changed to "children of the living God.")

6. Have a class member read aloud the small article, "Worship of Baal," in the *Study Guide.* Lead members to respond to this question: *What are some gods people worship today rather then the one true living God?* (Sports, money, cars, etc.) Record answers on the board.

7. Form two groups and give them the following assignments. Call for reports after about five minutes.

    *   *Group one*: Read Hosea 2:2–5 and discover what the conditions were for the relationship to be restored (unfaithfulness must end, etc.).
    *   *Group two*: Read Hosea 2:6–13 and discover what disciplines God would bring on Israel to get them to return and be faithful to him.

8. In advance, on a poster board, list the things God would do to restore the relationship with Israel (2:14–23). Use a hidden poster. That is, cover each point and reveal it as you are ready to discuss that point. These points could be:

    *   The Lord pursues the wandering one with tenderness.
    *   The unfaithful will be restored to faithfulness.
    *   A new peace and safety will be renewed.
    *   Righteousness, justice, love, mercy, and faithfulness characterize the restored relationship.

9. Read 3:1–5 aloud while the class listens for the Lord's instruction to Hosea and how this illustrates God's love for Israel. Lead the class to consider God's relationship to Israel and Hosea's relationship to Gomer. Note that God was seeking to bring Israel into a restored relationship. Explain these verses from information in the *Study Guide* and in "Bible Comments" in this *Teaching Guide.*

Encourage Application

10. Before class prepare and place around the room signs that say:

    • Strongly agree
    • Mildly agree
    • Mildly disagree
    • Strongly disagree

    Write the following question on the board: *Why have you been saved from your sin to a relationship with God?* Instruct the class that as you read each possible answer to the statement written on the board, they are to stand under one of the four signs that best describes how they feel about that answer. Read some of the following answers, one at a time, and allow the class members to move and stand under the sign that best represents their feeling. Have them share their reasons for selecting that sign to stand under. Here are some possible answers to the question:

    • To be a good church member and pay my tithes
    • To raise my children in the church so they will become faithful church members
    • To continue the ministry of Jesus Christ
    • To have correct doctrinal beliefs
    • To live a transformed lifestyle
    • To defend social and moral issues
    • To be on mission with God

11. In advance, ask a class member to be ready to read aloud from the *Study Guide* the small article, "Getting a Missional Perspective." Lead the class to take each of the three areas and discuss ways individuals or the class as a whole can move from believing into action concerning missions. List on the board the actions that the group agrees to take this next week.

12. Close with prayer for courage to become leaders in helping people become involved in these actions.

Teaching Plan—Lecture and Questions

Connect with Life

1. Ask: *Have you ever bought an old house or a piece of antique furniture and sought to restore it to its original state?* Invite members to share experiences.

2. State that God is in the business of restoration. He takes the initiative to mend the brokenness and make it whole again.

3. Use the story about George Truett found in the *Study Guide* or use one from personal experience to draw the class into the lesson.

Guide Bible Study

4. Refer to the first outline point from the *Study Guide*: "The Living God Turns Reality Downside Up (1:10—2:1)." Write it on the board. Ask: *What does God do to begin restoring a relationship? How does God turn reality downside up?* Point out that these verses help us with these questions.

5. Invite members to read Hosea 1:10—2:1 and find the answer to this question: *What do these verses tell us about how God related to Israel?* (God desired to restore the relationship and pursued them to make it happen.)

6. Refer to the second outline point, "The Agony of Victory (2:2–5)." Encourage members to read this passage and look for answers to this question: *What kind of God do you see in these verses?* Call for responses, and then ask: *What conditions did God put on the people to restore the relationship?* (Israel had to return and be faithful.)

7. Refer to the third outline point, "Hidden in Plain Sight (2:14–23)." Refer to the George Truett story again, and explain what he had to do so he could follow God's will. Have a member read verses 14–23 and ask the class to listen for answers to this question: *What would*

happen when God restored his relationship with Israel? Call for responses. As needed, summarize briefly the meaning of these verses, emphasizing God's promise and plan to restore Israel and the blessings that would come.

8. Refer to the fourth outline point, "A Love That Will Not Stop (3:1–2)." Read these verses aloud. Explain these verses by sharing thoughts from the *Study Guide* and from "Bible Comments" in this *Teaching Guide.* Consider what these verses suggest about God's love for us.

9. Refer to the fifth outline point, "Saved From, To, and For (3:3–5)." Read these verses aloud. Emphasize the restoration to serve him again that God was going to provide after a time of discipline. Ask: *What are you saved from? What are you saved to? What are you saved for?* Encourage the class to answer in light of these verses.

Encourage Application

10. Use these questions to guide thought and discussion on the implications of this lesson:

   • Do think there is ever a time when a relationship is not worth restoring? Why?
   • What relationships with our family, friends, and class members do we need to seek to restore? How can these relationships be restored?
   • How can we be used of God to help others learn how to restore their broken relationships with God, their family, or their friends?

Focal Text

Hosea 4:1–12; 8:1–10, 14

Background

Hosea 4—8

Main Idea

Religious beliefs and practices can transform a society for the good or lead it into evil.

Question to Explore

How should faithfulness to God be demonstrated in our day?

Teaching Aim

To lead the class to describe parallels between our practices and God's charges against Israel and identify implications for action

HOSEA

A God Who Judges and Restores

Lesson Eight

God's Charges

BIBLE COMMENTS

Understanding the Context

Whereas an understanding of the prophet's personal and family life are crucial to interpreting the first three chapters, the situation is not mentioned in the rest of the book. There are no more references to Gomer or to Hosea's children as they no longer play a role in illustrating the message from Yahweh. Thus, chapter 4 begins a new section in which Hosea speaks to the nations of Israel and Judah over a period of several years. Truth now comes from the prophet's messages, not his marriage. His remarks relating to the problems with society and religion do, however, require some understanding of the background and customs of that day.

Chapter 4 is written in the form of a covenant lawsuit in which God brought specific charges against Israel. This indictment of the people's sin may have been delivered at the city gates, where various leaders, including religious leaders, would assemble to discuss current issues. The presence of the priests would explain Hosea's lengthy pronouncements on those whom most would never speak against. God was obviously tired of the games and hypocrisy of those who supposedly represented him to the

85

people. Hosea's remarks to the priests are stern reminders to all in Christian leadership today.

In chapters 5—7, Hosea speaks of the nation's sexual sins, ritualism, dishonesty, deceitfulness, political corruption, and foreign policy. The Israelites had convinced themselves that as long as they offered their sacrifices, God would be happy with them. Of course, God is always interested in our hearts as well as our deeds. The rituals meant nothing as long as the people lived in sin and remained unrepentant.

Chapter 8 begins a section in which God makes very clear that Israel would reap the consequences of its sin. Israel's recurring infatuation with the gods of Canaan could no longer be tolerated. Their moral, ethical, and religious failures would result in their destruction. An agricultural principle is used in a familiar verse from this passage. While the Northern Kingdom planted "the wind," they would harvest a dangerous, violent storm (8:7). Their harvest would destroy them.

Interpreting the Scriptures

No Love = More Crime (4:1–3)

4:1–2. The opening phrase sounds like a summons for the people to appear before the great judge and hear the case against them. The charge is given both in terms of what was lacking and what was in abundance. What was lacking were the basics of following God, namely, faithfulness, love, and simple acknowledgement of God. The word "love" is from a Hebrew word rich in meaning. Among other possible translations are such words as "mercy" (KJV), "loyalty" (NRSV), or "kindness" (NASB). The word refers to that which is basic for maintaining a relationship. One way of acknowledging God is demonstrating faithfulness and love to him and to our fellow human beings. This was not happening during Hosea's time. What there was plenty of, however, was cursing, lying, murder, stealing, and adultery. This charge includes breaking half of the Ten Commandments.

4:3. All of creation was affected by the people's sins. Our actions, including disobedience to God, have a direct impact on the environment.

More Priests = More Sin (4:4–12)

4:4–5. Sin was so widespread that there was no room for finger-pointing. Everyone was guilty. However, God held the priests especially accountable for the condition of the nation. The reference to stumbling "by day" and "by night" is a way of saying they were always stumbling, being tripped up by their own poor leadership. The so-called "prophets" were being tripped as well. Those who should have recognized the flagrant sins of the people didn't notice because they were tripping over themselves in their own sin. The unusual reference to destroying their mother may indicate the end of the priestly line. Priests would cease to have sons to continue the tradition.

4:6–7. Part of the priest's duty was to teach others about God. The mention of "lack of knowledge" suggests they had ceased to do so. This would be one of the reasons the nation would fall. The reference to ignoring the children of priests would again suggest that the priestly lineage would soon cease. Since priests were no longer doing what God expected of them, God had no further use for them. In referencing the lack of future offspring, God pointed out that there were too many priests as it was, and all of them were corrupt. The more priests there were, the more sin there seemed to be in the land.

4:8–9. The priests were so corrupt that they had an appetite for more sin. They no longer had a conscience that made them feel shame and guilt for their actions. In fact, the more the people sinned, the more the priests seemed to profit from that sin. While previous verses indicate that wicked priests influenced the people, verse 9 indicates that the wicked people also influenced the priests. Regardless of who was to blame, both would be punished.

4:10–12. Although the religious leaders might actually be eating more because of the people's sin, they would always be hungry. Likewise, impotence among the priests was also a punishment. The analogy, while crude to our ears today, points out the sexual sins of the priests. More than likely, this is a reference to the worship of Baal, which involved sexual practices that were nothing more than adultery and fornication. Those whose life's vocation was to serve God were actively serving idols. Part of this behavior was fueled by the effects of alcohol. Indeed, sexual sin and alcohol abuse often go hand in hand. The priests were just as susceptible to that deadly combination as the laypeople. The same susceptibility is true of all clergy today.

Whether verse 12 is saying the people consulted a wooden idol or the priests themselves sought guidance from a carved image, it can be said that both were led away by a "spirit of prostitution." The spiritual adultery of the people, as already addressed by Hosea's marriage to Gomer, is the primary reason for the harsh judgment. Both the priests and the people were guilty.

Idols = Broken Covenant (8:1–6)

8:1. Like the robot in the old TV series, *Lost in Space*, who was always saying "Danger, danger, danger," the warning of impending doom in this verse is quite clear. Sometimes the trumpet was used as a rallying cry to bring encouragement. However, here it becomes an alarm, warning of the coming Assyrians. More than likely, this reference to the eagle points to the invading army that would be used by God as instruments of his punishment. The NRSV translates the Hebrew word as "vulture." The invasion of the Assyrians in 922 BC would soon fulfill this prophecy.

The Assyrian invasion would be the result of Israel's sin and rebellion. While there are many historical reasons Israel was conquered, it was ultimately because God allowed this portion of God's people to be destroyed because they, not God, had broken the covenant.

8:2–3. Even though the people cried out and answered the charge that they had not acknowledged God, it was merely words not supported by actions. It is human nature to deny such serious charges against us, particularly in the face of such a disaster. However, their hollow words would have no effect in avoiding the eagle (or vulture) circling ahead. Their days were already numbered. The language of verse 3 reminds us that it was Israel's choice to reject the good. Similarly, we are all responsible for our actions. When we follow a pathway of disobedience, we will find our enemies right behind us.

8:4–6. Another of the specific charges against Israel relates to the political process of selecting the king and the way in which the king ruled. One of the things almost every king of Israel did in defiance of God was to encourage the worship of idols. The "idols" refers to the calf-idols of Samaria that sat at Dan and Bethel (1 Kings 12:28–31). These idols made with precious metals would soon lead to the nation's destruction. There is a play on words in verse 5. The same word used in verse 3 to describe Israel's rejection of what is good is used in verse 5 to describe God's rejection of their idols. Verse 6 reminds the people that the images are from them, from their hands, not God. These idols would one day be broken. The same is true of our idols today. They are man-made and thus very fragile.

Sowing Sin = Reaping Judgment (8:7–10, 14)

8:7–8. Verse 7 is one of the most famous passages from Hosea. The agricultural principle is that one reaps what one sows (see Galatians 6:7). The principle is simply that one does not harvest grapes when one plants wheat. The idea from Hosea is that one harvests something much bigger than what one sowed. A whirlwind is significantly stronger and more dangerous than a wind. Likewise, even though Israel might think its sins were small and insignificant, they had best be prepared for what they were about to harvest.

Their harvest, which by one measure might be large, would not be worth anything. This is an example of having a lot of something but having nothing of any value. Even if what Israel planted were to grow, it would be devoured by the enemies. The harvest was of no profit. Israel would be blown away by what they had done. Israel was as worthless to God as a field of grain with no head. If, as speculated earlier, the land was experiencing a drought during this time, the imagery would have been even more powerful.

8:9–10. Israel had a history of paying tribute to the Assyrians in an attempt to buy their protection and favor. King Menaham collected silver from every wealthy Israelite and gave it to the Assyrians to keep them from attacking (2 Kings 15:19). When the king went "up to Assyria" for help, as opposed to going to God, their help turned on them. In reality, the nation was as alone as a donkey. The reference to Ephraim was another way of referring to the Northern Kingdom.

Israel also paid tribute to the Egyptians. However, regardless of how many nations Israel turned to for help, Israel was betrayed by them all and considered worthless as an ally. The mighty king referred to in verse 10 is more than likely Tiglath-Pileser, the King of Assyria. God looked on Israel's failed foreign policy as further proof of Israel's refusing to trust in him.

8:14. This summary statement says that Israel was guilty of forgetting God. The references to palaces and fortified towns reminds us of the human tendency to place our faith and trust in what we can build and accomplish rather than in God. Materialism, a huge problem today, was also prevalent during Hosea's time. The reference to Judah, the Southern Kingdom, served as a sober reminder that they too must repent of their sins before they were punished as severely as Israel.

Focusing on the Meaning

While we would prefer to read of God's grace and goodness, we must remind ourselves that God does punish sin. Israel had gone too far and ignored too many warning signs. By this point in Hosea's career, there was no chance left for Israel.

Many of the sins mentioned in Hosea are relevant today. Sexual sin, disobedience, placing trust in others instead of God, spiritual adultery, and ignoring God's will even in our political choices are just a few examples. Forgetting God, even while being blessed by God, is a real possibility. Indeed, America may one day have to reap the whirlwind and face destruction and punishment for our many sins.

Those in Christian leadership are certainly not perfect. However, they must hold themselves to the highest standard and be constantly aware that their spiritual condition influences others. Judgment would come on Israel because of the sins of religious and political leaders.

Materialism contributed to Israel's downfall. Materialism in America is basically the same as idolatry. While most Americans do not have a statue of some mythological deity in their home, they do have things, bought with their money, that they revere and cherish more than they honor God. Even in churches, we tend to make idols out of buildings and programs. We routinely bow down to them without much thought.

The messages of Hosea contain images and illustrations intended to get the attention of the audience. The message was critical. How is God trying to get your attention today? Are there warning signs relating to sin in your life? Are you listening to God's message? In what areas in your life might you be disobeying God and how does such behavior affect those around you?

TEACHING PLANS

Teaching Plan—Varied Learning Activities

Connect with Life

1. Begin by reading 2 Chronicles 7:14 to the class. Ask: *Is the United States a nation that humbles itself before God?* Call for the class to share some examples. Continue by asking: *What differences would we see in the United States if we were people who followed God?*

2. Summarize Hosea 1—3 and preview briefly where chapter 4 and the following chapters will take us. (See *Study Guide* under "When God Complains" and "Understanding the Context" in this *Teaching Guide*). State that today's lesson deals with charges being brought by God against Israel.

Guide Bible Study

3. In advance, set your classroom up like a courtroom, with a place for the judge, witnesses, and jury. Early in the week, enlist class members to role-play the following parts:

   - Prosecuting attorney to present the case against Israel
   - Prosecuting attorney to present the case against the church today
   - Bailiff (who reads each complaint)
   - Two witnesses (Optional)

   These are the speaking parts. As the teacher you will serve as the judge, directing the trial. Several class members can sit in the jury box (also optional). Participants should review "When God Complains (4:1–12)" in the *Study Guide* for ideas. Use additional information from Hosea 4—7 as needed. A rehearsal of the speaking parts during the week or early before class time on Sunday will be needed.

4. Deal with each complaint separately. The bailiff will read the complaint, and then the prosecuting attorneys will ask questions while

the witnesses give testimony. (Or the prosecuting attorneys can present the evidence instead of using witnesses.)

5. The verdict is rendered in 8:1–10, 14. As the judge, read the verdict to the class, or select a member of the jury to serve as foreman and read the verdict. (*Your honor we find the defendant. . . .*)

   (*An alternate suggestion for steps 3–5*: Instead of using the trial format, enlist one member to do a monologue of the information. As teacher, read each complaint, and have the member present all of the other information in a monologue. Or you could enlist two members to help, one reading the information about Israel's day, and the other for the church today.)

Encourage Application

6. Ask: *What needs to happen in our country and in our personal lives if we are to be declared not guilty by the judge?* Continue discussion by asking question 5 from the *Study Guide*. Then ask, *What difference would it make in our lives or our country if we really humbled ourselves before God today?*

Teaching Plan—Lecture and Questions

Connect with Life

1. Write on the board or a tear sheet a heading with these words: *People who are faithful.* On the left side of the sheet (board), lead the class to list Bible characters who demonstrated true faithfulness. On the right side of the sheet, lead members to list some people in today's world whom they would consider faithful to God.

2. Inquire: *How would you define the word, faithfulness?* Be prepared to share a definition, or bring a dictionary and ask a member to read the definition to the class.

Guide Bible Study

3. Refer to the Question to Explore, "How should faithfulness to God be demonstrated in our day?"

4. Summarize from the *Study Guide* the information concerning Hosea and what we learned about him from chapters 1—3 and what we are going to discover about him in chapters 4 and following.

5. Remind the class that the people of Israel had been very unfaithful to God. State that as we study our Scripture for today, we need to look for the parallels between Israel in that day and our churches today.

6. Ask: *Do you like to receive complaints from another person? What if those complaints are valid?* State that we are going to discover the complaints God had against Israel.

7. In advance, from the *Study Guide*, prepare a handout sheet with the four complaints printed on them (see under "When God Complains). Leave enough space between each complaint for the members to make notes.

8. Enlist a class member to read Hosea 4:1 aloud. After the reading, state the first complaint God had. Using the *Study Guide*, explain what Israel was doing to bring about this complaint.

9. Ask: *Do people come to church more for fellowship than to worship God? What do you think is the real reason people come to church today? What evidence do we see of people not being faithful to God?* (Note the question found in the *Study Guide* under complaint #1.) *Is it possible that people are going to church for entertainment and social purposes instead of for worshiping God?*

10. Invite a member to read 4:2 aloud, and to state the second complaint God had against Israel. Using the *Study Guide*, explain what Israel was doing to bring about this complaint. Ask: *What were some of the things God was accusing Israel of doing? Are these prevalent in today's churches? How are we breaking God's laws today?*

11. Select a member to read 4:3 aloud. State the third complaint God had against Israel. Using the *Study Guide*, explain what Israel was doing to bring about this complaint. Ask: *How much should the church be involved in keeping the environment clean? Does the church need to teach the children and youth to enjoy and preserve the beauty that God has created for us? Are the adults in our church setting the right example?*

12. Enlist a member to read 4:4–12 aloud and to state the fourth complaint God had against Israel. Using the *Study Guide*, explain what Israel was doing to bring about this complaint. Be sure to mention that the religious leaders of Israel were corrupt, telling lies, being unfaithful to God, and pretending to be religious. Ask question 4 from the *Study Guide*.

13. From 8:1–10, 14, list on the board the warnings God gave Israel. Point out that if they continued in the way they were going, they would surely bring about their own doom. Provide additional information as needed from the *Study Guide* and from "Bible Comments" on these verses in this *Teaching Guide*.

Encourage Application

14. Ask question 5 and then question 2 from the *Study Guide*.

15. Refer the class to the small article in the *Study Guide* titled, "Thirteen Ways to Nurture Your Relationship with God." Encourage the class to begin using at least one of these ways this week.

Focal Text

Hosea 11:1–11

Background

Hosea 9:1—11:11

Main Idea

In spite of their sins against him, God does not give up on people but yearns to show mercy to them.

Question to Explore

When we have sinned, does God want us back?

Teaching Aim

To lead the class to identify implications of God's not giving up on Israel in spite of their sins against him

H O S E A

A God Who Judges and Restores

Lesson Nine

God's Yearning Heart

BIBLE COMMENTS

Understanding the Context

Although the message in chapter 11 is one of hope and encouragement, it is in the context of the previous chapters that deal with God's punishment and wrath. In just the previous two chapters, predictions of everything from unproductive farmland to the end of the monarchy have been pronounced. In chapters 9—10 Israel was told that judgment was coming. They would be forced to live in Assyria where they would not be able to adhere to their unique dietary customs (9:3). The altars used for idolatry would be destroyed (10:1–2), and the nation would experience the horrors of war (10:13–15).

A reference in 10:5 to the "calf-idol of Beth Aven" provides some insight to the extent of the Northern Kingdom's idolatry. Evidently this idol was so revered and cherished that when the Assyrian king carried it away, the Israelites would be devastated (10:6). It is hard for us to imagine that hundreds of years after the Exodus, God's people were still making and worshiping statues of calves. How ironic that in order to get their full attention with the coming judgment, God would have to remove that which was the reason for the judgment in the first place. The extent of their spiritual adultery was that bad.

While the metaphor of a husband and wife has dominated this book so far, the image changes in chapter 11 to that of a parent and child. God is depicted as a nurturing and loving Father. His compassion and mercy become the new theme. This is a welcome change for today's reader who by this point likely has tired of the language of wrath. By alluding to Israel's past and God's ever-present love, there is hope for today and tomorrow. Indeed, such a message of hope is needed by these who are about to be punished for their idolatry. It is a much needed message today as well.

Interpreting the Scriptures

Desertion (11:1–4)

11:1. While the image of a husband and wife speaks to the love that God has for his people, the image of a parent and child speaks more to God's commitment and dedication, particularly in light of marriage and family relationships in the Old Testament era. Referring to Israel as his son, God invoked the image of a loving, caring father who was willing to make any sacrifice necessary for one of his children. The implication from this verse is that Israel was no longer a child but had grown to be an adult. However, as is sometimes the case with grown children today, physical maturity does not equate maturity in other ways. Obviously Israel was acting in a childish manner. The reference to the Exodus from Egypt served to remind the Jews that their whole existence as a nation was the result of God's grace and goodness. Matthew saw Messianic implications in this verse when he quoted it in Matthew 2:15.

11:2. The word "called" in verses 1–2 reminds us of a parent calling his or her child in from the neighborhood after a long day of summer play. However, just as children do not always heed their parents call ("I didn't hear you!"), Israel went further from God. Verse 2 reinforces the idea that God was not moving away from the rebellious child. Rather the child was moving further away from God. This movement was evident in Israel's turning to other gods.

11:3. Any parents who actively helped their child learn to stand and then take the first steps can identify with God's patience and love as pictured in verse 3. Israel had a lot of growing to do after leaving Egypt. Their

Heavenly Father was there all the way. As Israel took the first baby steps and moved on to the independent movements of an adolescent, God was always willing to hold their hand and walk with them. However, like a child who feels he or she is too big to hold a parent's hand while crossing the street, Israel took advantage of their new independence and did as they pleased.

11:4. While some see verse 4 as a continuation of the parent/child analogy, others see a shift to an agricultural metaphor where Israel is compared to an ox. The images of leading an animal with a cord or rope, removing a yoke, and feeding them speak to a kind and gentle farmer caring for an animal. The word "neck" can be translated "jaw" (NASB; "jaws" in KJV). Of course, a yoke is placed around the animal's shoulder. However, the word "yoke" is one vowel different from the word "infant." If the word "infant" was intended, the phrase could refer to lifting an infant to one's cheek or jaw, as the New Revised Standard Version translation indicates. Such an image is certainly in keeping with the thoughts of 11:1–3. Regardless of the image intended, the central truth of God's gentleness and compassion remain unchanged. Whether Israel was like a child who needed love or like a farm animal that needed training, God was ready to provide whatever care and attention were needed. God is a God of love and kindness.

Punishment (11:5–7)

11:5. Just as any responsible parent knows that disobedient children need discipline, so God knew that Israel must be punished. The "return to Egypt" refers to the bondage endured while in Egypt, not a return to that particular geographical area. The term "Egypt" symbolized living in a foreign land. Since Israel had refused to stop worshiping idols, and thereby had forfeited their relationship with God, they must now forfeit the land. The land and freedom were gifts that they had abused. The deliverance from Egypt to their own land must now be reversed.

11:6. The bondage would come from the Assyrians. Indeed, the slow takeover by the Assyrian Empire had more than likely already begun. An economic crisis had developed because of the large amounts of extortion money paid to the enemy. Soon the Assyrians would demand more than just tribute money. They would actually invade the Northern Kingdom. The flashing of swords and destruction of fortified gates would lead to a complete takeover. Whatever future plans the leaders had made with other countries would mean absolutely nothing. While many of Israel's kings thought they could buy some time with the Assyrians or enter into some kind of treaty, the aggressor thought of only invasion and destruction. According to verse 5, all of this would happen because God's people had refused to repent.

11:7. Even as the enemy had already begun seizing some of the outlying areas, the people stubbornly continued in their sin. The reference to the Most High can be taken in two different ways. The capitalization of the phrase in the NIV conveys the idea that when the people cried out to God, God would not hear. However, the phrase may also refer to the high places where other gods were worshiped. Those other gods would not respond to their cries. Either way, it is a precarious predicament when a nation has no one to hear their cries for help.

Compassion (11:8–9)

11:8. The Father's love could not completely give up on his child Israel. It was not in God's character. God was pondering the dilemma between judgment and mercy. The questions seem to indicate a divine struggle. God knew what Israel deserved, and yet God knew how much he loved his people. This love is the source of his compassion that is "aroused" or excited. The phrase means that all God's compassions had come together. Obviously, God's compassions outweighed God's anger.

The two cities mentioned, Admah and Zeboiim, were destroyed with Sodom and Gomorrah (Deuteronomy 29:23). This incident reminds one of what God's anger can do. The difference this time, however, was the unique relationship, like that of a father and son, that God had with his chosen people. Just as Hosea continued to love his unfaithful wife, so God, because of his character, must continue to love unfaithful Israel. The tension between punishment and love is always hard to understand.

11:9. The phrase in which God reminds us that he is not like human beings has meaning for parents of grown children today. Sometimes parents give up on their children. After enduring the same kind of heartache and rejection that God had experienced, parents may completely disown one of their offspring. This is a natural, human response. However, God said he was not like that. In spite of his "fierce anger," God still considered the wayward son his son. The fact that God is not like human beings answers many of the questions we have about why God acts as he does in certain situations. We know how we might react and can explain our rationale. However, God is God. His way is best.

Perhaps someone enrolled in your Bible study rarely attends because he or she feels God has given up on them. Perhaps he or she has been rejected by a parent in the past and thus feels rejected by God as well. This chapter of Hosea could be especially meaningful to them as it conveys the love of God.

Homecoming (11:10–11)

After describing how Israel had walked away from him, God now says that one day his people will follow him. The metaphor changes to the animal kingdom, where God's majesty and power is compared to the lion and Israel's timidity is compared to that of a dove. Whereas the people had become disobedient and obstinate, they would one day recognize where they stand when compared to Yahweh. The contrast between a lion and a dove seems appropriate to describe the differences between people and God. Indeed, all people should tremble when they encounter "the Holy One" (11:9).

The imagery of the birds also reminds one of birds returning to their nest. God says that he "will settle them in their homes." The Jews of the Northern Kingdom never returned from Assyria, however. When the city of Samaria finally fell to the Assyrians in 722/721 BC, 27, 290 Israelites (according to the Assyrian King, Sargon II) were deported to Upper Mesopotamia never to be heard from again. The small group of Israelites who remained intermarried with captives from other nations who were resettled in Israel (see 2 Kings 17:24). The descendants of these marriages became the Samaritans mentioned in the New Testament.

Perhaps verse 11 refers to the Jews of the Southern Kingdom returning home from Babylonian captivity 200 years later. This remnant would of course provide the world with the Jewish line that ultimately gave birth to the Messiah. Another view is that this prophecy simply refers to a time in which Jews would once again be an independent state. Still another idea is that fulfillment will come one day when Jews will enter the kingdom of God. Still others argue that all of the promises and prophecies relating to Israel have been transferred to the New Testament church.

Regardless of the interpretation one chooses, the central truth of God's love and compassion can not be denied. Even through his anger, God still allowed the prophesied Messiah to come and offer salvation to all the peoples of the world.

Focusing on the Meaning

A helpful exercise for people who feel as if their sin is more than God can forgive is to read this chapter of Hosea, substituting their name for every reference to Israel. This provides a personal sense of God's love and concern for us as individuals even when our lifestyle does not reflect God's will. While there may be questions regarding the fulfillment of this passage for the inhabitants of the Northern Kingdom, there is no doubt as to the message of grace and hope for Christians today. God's love never quits. The truths from these verses speak volumes of what it means to be able to call the Creator "our Father."

The story of the father waiting for his "prodigal" son to return home is a powerful New Testament image of God's unconditional love for us (see Luke 15:11–24). This chapter of Hosea is a similarly powerful image from the Old Testament. We are prone, like the prodigal son and the Northern Kingdom, to run away from God. He is prone, like a loving Father, to woo us back. It is part of God's nature to patiently wait on us. With arms open wide, God waits for his repentant children to come home.

If your Bible study group has found the study of Hosea to be somewhat depressing, this lesson offers hope. The images of a parent teaching a child to walk and of a grown child rebelling against his or her parents are powerful images to which many can relate. This lesson has something to say about how we parent, discipline, and love. It also has something to say about how we obey and remain devoted to our heavenly Father. This lesson may also provide discussion about earthly fathers who are not as tender and compassionate as God is.

Are we as ready to forgive as God is? Are our relationships with others marked by compassion and mercy? Those who may not have found themselves running away from God can still find truths in this passage that apply to their lives today. God has qualities that we are to try to imitate. Taking a cue from God, we should not give up on others who have let us down. Love should be waiting around every corner of despair and rejection. Restoration should always be an option.

TEACHING PLANS

Teaching Plan—Varied Learning Activities

Connect with Life

1. Begin with the following case study, or use one from your experience:

   Tom and Mary were Christian parents who sought to teach their Christian values to their children. Their teenage daughter was tired of rules that she thought were too strict. She began to rebel by doing things that were not pleasing to her parents. She began smoking, drinking, and experimenting with drugs. She also began breaking curfew and refusing to go to church, attending only when forced to go. She got in trouble at school, her grades dropped, and it seemed no punishment given by her parents worked. One night she came home very late and was drunk. The next day her parents told her that she was going to have to change her ways and obey the rules of their house, or she would have to leave. They were concerned about her actions and about her influence on their two younger children.

   The next night she did not come home until breakfast. They told her that she could not come in. She left, and they did not hear from her for six months. All during this time they continued to pray for her. One night the phone rang and it was their daughter calling. She had nowhere to go, her money had run out, her friends had dumped her, and she was sick and hungry. She called and asked them to help her. They brought her back home, nursed her to health, and began the process of helping her restore her life.

2. State that this case study is how God and Israel's relationship was in today's lesson. Israel was rebellious and had turned away from God. God continued to love them and wanted to bring them back into a relationship with him.

Guide Bible Study

3. Form small groups to review Hosea 9—10. Each group is to search for the following information:

   - How God thought of Israel
   - How God was going to punish Israel
   - What the prophet said to them

   Assign each group one of the following Scriptures to study: Hosea 9:1–9; Hosea 9:10–17; Hosea 10:1–8; Hosea 10:9–15.

   Make any combination of Scriptures to fit the needs of the groups in your class. After a few minutes, ask for each group to report their findings. Provide each group with a tear sheet and a marker to use in recording their findings. Have them place their sheet on the wall as they give their report.

4. In advance ask several class members to bring a family picture and be ready to share with the class a favorite memory. After their time of sharing, ask: *What pictures can we find of God in Hosea 11:1–4?* Enlist someone to read this passage aloud. Call for responses to the question. Emphasize how God remembered Israel as a child and how the image of God as a loving Father was very difficult for Israel to accept. (See *Study Guide* under "Parental Memories.") Then share that sometimes parental memories are not always pleasant.

5. Have the class think back to the case study. Ask: *How do you feel about the way the parents handled their rebellious daughter?* Refer to their reports on how God was going to punish Israel. Note that it was because they had turned away from a faithful, loving relationship that punishment came.

6. Summarize briefly 11:5–7.

7. In advance, have a class member ready to report on 11:8–11. Or plan to do a mini-lecture on what the passage teaches about what God really felt about Israel. Make sure to point out God's love and his threefold declaration as found in verse 9 (see *Study Guide*).

Encourage Application

8. Refer again to the case study and ask: *What are some ways our class, or we as individuals, can minister to a family that is hurting because of a rebellious child?*

9. Ask: *How can our church demonstrate that God hates the sin but always loves the sinner and is willing to help to restore a faithful relationship?*

Teaching Plan—Lecture and Questions

Connect with Life

1. Write this statement on the board: *Love means you never have to say you are sorry.* Ask: *Do you agree or disagree with this statement? Why?*

2. Continue the discussion by asking: *How are we to respond to and treat people who reject our love?* State that in today's lesson we will discover that God did not give up on Israel in spite of their rebellion against him.

Guide Bible Study

3. Refer to the first outline point from the *Study Guide*: "Be Sure Your Sin Will Find You Out (9:1—10:15)." Summarize the punishment that God would bring on Israel (see *Study Guide*). Point out that Hosea in his preaching called on Israel to seek the Lord, and emphasize what Israel's reaction was to God.

4. Refer to the second outline point: "Parental Memories (11:1–4)." Invite the class to share some pleasant memories from their childhood and from their parenting. State that not all childhood and parental memories are pleasant. Invite members to share an experience when they knew they were not in God's will for their life. Ask: *How did you know you were not in God's will? What was your response to God at that time?*

5. Summarize the information in the *Study Guide* on verses 1–4, showing God's remembrances and how Israel responded to God's love for them.

6. Refer to the third outline point, "Parental Frustration (11:5–7)." Ask: *Is there ever a time when a parent needs to say "that's enough"? If so, what should a parent do? What finally caused God to say enough is enough to Israel?* (See 11:7.) Review verses 5–7 so the class can understand why God was saying enough was enough.

7. Refer to the fourth outline point, "The Heart of God (11:8–9)." Encourage members to read verses 8–9 and think about how they would paraphrase these verses in today's language as if it were a parent speaking to a wayward child. Call for responses. Point out that these two verses reveal the real character of God (love).

8. Using information from the *Study Guide*, refer to the three-fold declaration of God's intent as found in verse 9.

9. Point out that the fifth outline point is "The Homecoming (11:10–11)." Compare the differences between rebellion and homecoming as found in these verses. Use information from the *Study Guide* under this outline point as needed.

Encourage Application

10. Review with the class the information found in the *Study Guide* under the heading "Implications for Today."

11. Ask question 1 from the *Study Guide*, followed by question 5. Have the class list ways that they can become involved this week in carrying out the responses to this question.

Focal Text

Hosea 14

Background

Hosea 11:12—14:9

Main Idea

God offers restoration and abundant new life to people who return to him.

Question to Explore

What hope is there when the sentence is "guilty as charged"?

Teaching Aim

To lead the class to decide how they will respond to God's invitation to return to him

HOSEA

A God Who Judges and Restores

Lesson Ten

Return to the Lord

BIBLE COMMENTS

Understanding the Context

In Hosea 12, God once again reviewed Israel's sin. This time, however, God did so using Jacob as an example. In many ways, Israel was acting like their deceiving patriarch (Hosea 12:2–4). Jacob's name literally means *he grasps the heel* (a reference to his birth story; see Genesis 25:26) and thus figuratively means *he deceives.* One could not hear the name Jacob without remembering his deceptive practices with his twin brother, even from birth. Jacob's descendants to whom Hosea wrote were guilty of deceiving others in the marketplace and of deceiving themselves by making futile alliances with Egypt and Assyria. The people had also tried to deceive God with their sacrifices at Gilgal. However, God was not mocked. He said that he would "repay him according to his deeds" (Hosea 12:2).

Hosea 12:6 outlines three things we must do today. Returning to God, preserving love and justice, and waiting on God are all important steps in personal renewal. Love and justice are the first qualities to suffer when people become deceitful. The Israelites no longer cared for their fellow human beings. Many times, moreover, deceit is the result of not having patience with

God. Instead of waiting for God's timing, we try to manipulate others in order to achieve our goals.

The next chapter offers more clues as to the extent of idolatry in the Northern Kingdom. Silver was used to construct the images, and the calf was still the idol of choice (13:2). God's people had sunk to the very depths of idolatry and sin. As a result, God said that their lives would become as brief as mist, dew, chaff, or smoke (13:3). If you worship nothing, you get nothing, and you become nothing.

In wrath, God would turn on them like a wild animal (13:7). The images of being mauled by a wild beast were intended to frighten the idolaters. As a result, they would turn to their king for protection. However, the monarchy had let the people down. Those who now ruled were poor spiritual leaders and could offer no relief from God's wrath. As a result, the nation would be destroyed agriculturally, economically, and politically. As verse 16 says, "the people of Samaria must bear their guilt."

Interpreting the Scriptures

The Prophet's Word (14:1–2a)

14:1. Hosea's final call in this book was for Israel to "return" to God. The word is usually used to describe true repentance. It implies that a change has taken place in a person's life and that a "U-turn" is in order to get back on the right path and avoid future sin. This term does not allow for half-hearted apologies or lip service. Those who sin against God must change their ways. By turning to the Baals, Israel had turned its back on God. In light of all the charges brought by God in this book, the only appropriate action left for Israel was a complete about-face.

The people had "stumbled" (NRSV, NASB) or tripped because of their sin. The image of a father teaching his child to walk in chapter 11 reminds us that the child had taken off on its own and had fallen. Sin trips us up. Although the language speaks to the nation as one individual, thus emphasizing the corporate effect of sin, personal lives are also tripped up by sin. Many have found themselves flat on their face, both figuratively and literally, because of sin. However, the God who taught us to walk can help us get back on our feet. The direction we travel is our choice.

14:2a. Throughout the Bible, repentance involves more than just physical changes. It also involves verbalizing our repentance toward God. Hosea told the people they must return and "take words" with them. Repentance begins with confession, and confession involves appropriate language expressing our feelings about our sin. The words are not for God's sake. His acceptance of us when we repent is not based on what we say. The words are for our sake. When we hear ourselves agreeing with God that our actions are indeed hurtful to God and ourselves, it helps us determine to change those particular actions.

The People's Word (14:2b–3)

14:2b. Hosea stated what the people were to say as they approached God in repentance. While confession does not involve a formula or specific wording, certain elements are important in expressing our feelings about our sin. One such element would be actually to ask for forgiveness. The phrase "Forgive all our sins" is literally *lift up and bear away*. The word describes the removal of sin as symbolized by the scapegoat on the Day of Atonement (Leviticus 16:20–22). When we ask God for forgiveness, we are asking God to remove our sins from us.

Another element in confession includes recognizing God's grace. The phrase "receive us graciously" reminded the people that forgiveness was not something they deserved or had earned. It was by the grace of God. Although the concept of grace as we understand it today may not be as developed in the Old Testament, the people did have a sense of how undeserving they were. The phrase "fruit of our lips" may be intended as a promise of future praise from the people. A footnote in the NIV and the NRSV refers to the word for *calf* or *bull* that is in the Hebrew text. The phrase may suggest that the people were saying that the verbal praise once offered to their calf-idol would now be directed to God.

14:3. Confession must always be specific. Verse 3 is specific confession regarding three areas with which Israel had problems. They had placed their trust and confidence in (1) alliances with other nations rather than God; (2) their own military might ("war-horses"); and (3) the idols they had made. Such a confession was also a promise that they would now depend on God. True repentance involves more than just an admission of guilt. It should include a promise to change. It is interesting to note that the nation whom Israel thought would ultimately defend them was the nation that would destroy them. Many times, when we trust something more than God, God uses that very thing to punish us.

The last word in verse 3 is translated "compassion" in the NIV and "mercy" in other translations (NRSV, NASB, and KJV). An interesting contrast can be made between this word toward the end of the book and its antonym found at the beginning of the book. Remember the name Hosea gave his daughter, Lo-Ruhamah, which means *no mercy* (1:6)? The name was an indictment on the people and offered no hope for restoration. Now, as the book closes, the people express the hope they have in God that God does indeed provide mercy.

God's Word (14:4–8)

14:4. After the people confessed and repented, God responded. Israel's "waywardness," or faithlessness, required healing. Such a condition had taken its toll on every area of life. Now that repentance had been made, God would begin to "heal" them. This thought does not refer to a release from the consequences or punishment for their sin. However, it is an example of God's love. While God despises sin, God is still in love with the sinner. The phrase that God's anger had "turned away from them" is in indication that God had indeed heard their confession and forgiven their sins.

14:5. The reference to dew speaks of life and renewal. While in 13:3 it is an example of brevity, here it signifies refreshment. Just as Palestinian crops depend on the dew during the summer months, God's people can depend on him for spiritual nourishment. The lily is a plant that grows abundantly in Palestine. Its beauty was a sign of fertile soil. With God's blessings, people "blossom" and grow. The roots of a cedar tree provide an analogy as to the stability God provides during troubled times. The cedar is also known for its very pleasant fragrance. This quality also serves as a symbol of blessing.

14:6–7. Three times in verses 5–7 the verse ends with a reference to "Lebanon." This area was known for its luxuriant forests and rich soils. From its aromatic trees to its bountiful harvests, Lebanon was a symbol of blessings and abundance. With these metaphors, God was saying that he would, in a variety of ways, bless those who truly repent. Note that God's promises were relayed in agricultural terms with an emphasis on productive and fertile plants. The whole basis of Baal worship was to ensure timely rains and productive crops. God was saying that he alone could meet the people's needs.

14:8. Verse 8 presents several different possibilities for interpretation. While the KJV interprets the question as being asked by Israel (Ephraim), the NIV, NRSV, and NASB have the question being asked by God to Israel. Some commentators suggest there is dialogue here with the people saying lines 1 and 3 and God responding with lines 2 and 4. The context of the verse seems to indicate that God was doing all the talking. The footnote in the NIV makes the question even clearer. Some commentators suggest that God was asking, *Why put an idol next to me?* Likely, however, God was asking Israel why they should ever turn again to an idol in light of the fact that God could meet all their needs. God is the One who cares for us. Referring to himself as "a green pine tree," God was saying that he is constant, always in season. Whatever fruitfulness God's people experience is from above. *Why then,* God wonders, *would God's people have any need for calves and Baals?*

The Final Word (14:9)

The last verse is the prophet's summation of not just the final thoughts, but the whole book. Wisdom, according to Hosea, would be to understand and apply what has just been read. Hosea's message of judgment and repentance, although delivered in a rather unique way, was a message not to be just heard or read. Rather, one must "realize" and "understand" it. Perhaps Hosea's unorthodox means of delivering the message in the opening chapters caused many to have a hard time understanding the truth. Perhaps some were still so spiritually blind that they could not yet see their idolatry as sin. Hosea's concluding remarks indicate that it would take some serious contemplation in order to understand everything he had tried to say. Once Israel could agree with the Lord's assessment of their sin, then Israel would become wise.

Wisdom is needed today to understand the implications of the book. To disregard the book as having no relevance to the twenty-first century would be foolish. A wise person understands that we have problems with disobedience and idolatry and stand in need of repentance.

While men and women tend to think their ways are always right, that is not the case. God's ways are right. The word "right" means *straight* or *undeviating.* His ways do not change. Those who are righteous have no problem walking such a straight path. However, those who rebel and disobey God will "stumble" even on a straight path. They "stumble," of course, over their own sin. The word "stumble" continues the word picture painted by God in chapter 11 of a rebellious child walking away. Stumbling over the ways of the Lord is a good description of people who think they are doing right and somehow justify their sins in their minds. In the end, their hypocrisy will be their downfall.

Focusing on the Meaning

God expects us to repent of our sins by changing direction. God is not interested in apologies that are not accompanied by genuine change. He wants us to express our feelings of penitence and change the actions that initially led to the sin. The changes we make are just as important as the confession. In what area of your life do you need to make a "U-turn"?

God expects us to confess our sins verbally. Some may feel that confession is not necessary because "God knows everything." However, God desires that we verbalize our confession in order to help us understand the extent of the sin we are confessing. Confession is not telling God something God does not already know. Rather, it is agreeing with God that the deed or attitude is really a sin and breaks God's heart. Are there unconfessed sins in your life?

God expects us to rely solely on him. We are tempted to rely on many things and people. Some rely on money, technology, achievements, and positions, as well as on parents, spouses, and other significant people in their lives. Placing all of our dependence on anything or anyone other than God is wrong. Things and people let us down. God will never fail us. What are you relying on that is taking the place of God?

God wants to bless us. Our loving heavenly Father wants the very best for us. This is not to suggest, however, that God wants all of his children to be healthy and wealthy. That is not the intent of verses 5–7. In fact, many of God's blessings may at times not seem like blessings at all. However, God wants what he knows is best for us. Have you openly received all the blessings God has in store for you?

God expects us to heed God's word. God's word is given to us to read, study, and obey. While many who might attend your Bible study are good at reading and maybe even studying the Bible, obeying is the part with which we struggle. God gave us his word to change our lives. God's word causes us to want to repent and confess. It encourages us to rely on God and receive God's blessings. What have you learned from this study of Hosea that you need to apply in your life?

TEACHING PLANS

Teaching Plan—Varied Learning Activities

Connect with Life

1. In advance, have a class member make some road signs for display, including several signs that are blank.

2. Also in advance, enlist four members to role-play (act out) the story from the *Study Guide* about the two couples traveling together. At the beginning of the class, have the members present the role-play.

3. After the presentation, point out that the two women in the role-play felt the sincerity of the owners' inviting them to come back. Ask: *Have you ever received an invitation that you felt was insincere? How did you sense that the invitation was insincere?* Emphasize the sincerity of God's invitation to Israel.

Guide Bible Study

4. Refer to the road signs placed around the room. Invite members to tell what the signs say or mean. Ask: *What happens when you ignore these signs?* Note that Israel had many road signs that warned them of danger, but they ignored these signs.

5. Divide the class into two or more groups. Provide the following instructions: Find road signs Israel had ignored that warned them that they were going the wrong way and traveling away from God. Write these warnings on the blank road signs.

   - *Group 1.* Search Hosea 11:12—12:14. Assign a reporter to record the information and be ready to report.
   - *Group 2.* Search Hosea 13. Assign a reporter to record the information and be ready to report.

6. Have group 1 report using their signs, and read some of the warnings from the Scriptures. Add comments as needed.

7. Have group 2 report using their signs, and read the warnings from the Scriptures. Add comments as needed.

8. Summarize the information found in the *Study Guide* under the outline point, "Warning Signs on the Road Away from God."

9. Ask *Study Guide* question 2. In advance, have a class member ready to jump up and bark out the four military commands found in the *Study Guide* under the heading "Turn Around." Explain these commands from the information in the *Study Guide*.

10. Lead the class to list on the board things that we substitute today for true repentance (see "The Words of Repentance" in the *Study Guide*). Guide discussion of these substitutes.

11. In advance have a member ready to give a mini-lecture on the three images of God's character revealed in 14:4–5 (see the *Study Guide* under "How the Lord Responds to Repentance").

   • God as Healer
   • God as Lover
   • God as Life-giver

12. In advance, enlist a class member to be ready to read 14:5–8 aloud. Ask the class to listen for what God would do if Israel repented. Call for reports.

Encourage Application

13. Read the paraphrase of 14:9 under "The Sermon's Invitation" from the *Study Guide,* and ask the class to listen for the answer to this question: *What does this mean to us today?*

14. Ask question 1 from the *Study Guide*. Continue by asking question 3.

15. In closing, read aloud the small article titled "Think About It" from the *Study Guide*.

Teaching Plan—Lecture and Questions

Connect with Life

1. In advance make sure you have a dictionary in your classroom. To begin the class session, ask: *What do we mean when we say a church is going to have a revival? What do you think the word "revival" really means?* Enlist a class member to read the definition of the word *revival* from the dictionary.

2. Have a class member read the definition of the word *repentance* from the dictionary. State that in today's lesson we are going to discover some warning signs that revival and repentance are needed. Share that revival and repentance can bring change.

Guide Bible Study

3. Have a class member read Hosea 11:12—12:14 aloud. Ask the class to listen for warnings God was giving Israel about going the wrong way. Call for reports after the reading. Have a class member write responses on the board.

4. Enlist a class member to read Hosea 13. Ask the class to listen for more warnings that God was giving Israel about going the wrong way. Add to the responses on the board.

5. Ask the first portion of question 1 from the *Study Guide*: *Do you see any of the signs of Hosea's time among the people of God today?* Add, *Which ones?* Continue by asking: *Do you think we are doing a better job today of reading the warning signs than Israel did?* If the answer is *yes*, ask, *How?* If the answer is *no*, inquire, *Why aren't we?*

6. Continue: *With all of these warning signs, what did Israel need to do?* (Repent, be restored, experience revival, etc.) Read Hosea 14:1 aloud. Point out that God wanted Israel to turn around, to repent, to reclaim their relationship with him.

7. Read Albert Einstein's proverb from the *Study Guide* under the heading, "Turn Around." Ask: *Isn't this what we many times do today?* Encourage someone to share a personal example of this.

8. Read Hosea 14:2–3 aloud. Ask: *What is involved in true repentance to the Lord?* Refer to the statement in the *Study Guide* under the heading "The Words of Repentance" about one of the biggest temptations in modern Christianity. Ask: *What do people do today as a substitute for true repentance?* Ask without expecting an audible response: *How long has it been since you offered authentic words of repentance to the Lord?*

9. Read Hosea 14:4–7 aloud. Ask: *What words do you hear that reveal God's character to the people of God?* Refer to the ideas of God as Healer, Lover, and Life-giver under the heading, "How the Lord Responds to Repentance (14:4–5a),"in the *Study Guide*.

10. Read Hosea 14:8–9 aloud. Ask: *How can we experience repentance in our lives today?*

Encourage Application

11. Ask: *What are some warning signs we need to heed today?*

12. Comment on the small article in the *Study Guide* titled, "The Invitation." Remind the class that each week we need to search our lives, discover what warning signs have been placed along our path, and then respond to them in repentance.

13. Close the class with prayer, directing members to silently ask God to bring revival and true repentance into their hearts.

Where Coveting Leads

Focal Text
Micah 1:1–7; 2:1–9

Background
Micah 1—2

Main Idea
God judges people who oppress others in their desire to have more things for themselves.

Question to Explore
What place does the desire for things really have in your life?

Teaching Aim
To lead the class to relate God's condemnation of coveting to their life situation

MICAH

What the Lord Requires

BIBLE COMMENTS

Understanding the Context

Micah lived and prophesied in the same general time when Amos, Hosea, and Isaiah were living and delivering prophetic messages. While Amos and Hosea prophesied in Israel, Micah and Isaiah both lived in Judah, and most of their messages were directed there. Today Micah is less well-known than are his contemporary prophets, but such was probably not the case among the ancient Hebrews. A century later, Jeremiah said that the inspired preaching of Micah led to the saving of the city of Jerusalem from destruction (Jeremiah 26:18–19).

The book gives almost no personal information about Micah himself. His name is a shortened form of the word meaning, *Who is like Yahweh.* No word about his family appears. He prophesied in the times of three kings of Judah: Jotham, Ahaz, and Hezekiah; thus between 742 and 687 BC. No mention is made of a king of the Northern Kingdom of Israel, but since 1:1 states that Micah's vision included Samaria, his work must have begun before that city fell to the Assyrians. The focus of his work likely was from just before Samaria fell (722 BC) to just after Jerusalem was besieged but not captured by the Assyrian king, Sennacherib, in 701 BC.

Micah's hometown was Moresheth, a small town southwest of Jerusalem, not far from the old Philistine city of Gath. That he was no city dweller he makes clear in his messages. Sinful corruption centered in the cities. To Micah, cities were cesspools of iniquity. Micah longed for the purer life of the countryside and its villages. His contemporary, Isaiah, was at home in Jerusalem and its aristocratic circles, often advising kings. But Micah was at home in the villages and countryside. God had a place for each, and both served God well.

Micah witnessed and spoke concerning some momentous events in the life of the Hebrews. Assyrian power had become the dominant force in the biblical world when he began his prophetic ministry. Tiglath-Pileser III, sometimes called Pul in the Old Testament (2 Kings 15:19), was one of the great Assyrian kings in this time. He responded to a plea from Ahaz, king of Judah, in 732 BC, when Judah was threatened by a coalition of the kings of Israel and Syria. Tiglath-Pileser's response was to invade the areas north of Judah. He conquered Syria and reduced Israel to a vassal state ruled by Hoshea. Ten years later Hoshea rebelled, and Assyria, now ruled by Sargon II, conquered Israel and exiled thousands of their inhabitants. Through all of this time Judah had paid tribute to Assyria and thus had escaped military attacks.

Some years later, during Hezekiah's reign, Judah did face an Assyrian invasion, and many of her cities were destroyed. Sennacherib, the Assyrian ruler at the time, also besieged Jerusalem in 701 BC, but left the city unconquered after "the angel of the LORD set out and struck down one hundred eighty-five thousand in the camp of the Assyrians" (2 Kgs. 19:35) This was after the repentance and prayers of Hezekiah. This action of Hezekiah and Micah's encouragement must be what Jeremiah referred to in Jeremiah 26:18–19, as noted above. In the twentieth century, archaeologists discovered an inscription made at the order of Sennacherib, usually called "The Taylor Inscription." This inscription listed by name the many cities in Palestine Sennacherib destroyed on this 701 BC campaign. With no claim that he conquered Jerusalem, he boasted that he "shut Hezekiah up like a bird in a cage," but he never claimed to have taken the city. He did, however, claim that he took tribute payment from Hezekiah. Ancient inscriptions were mostly "brag" documents, written to boast of the great successes of the king. It is not surprising that Sennacherib would fail to mention a disaster that befell his army.

Interpreting the Scriptures

Judgment Against Jerusalem and Samaria (1:2–7)

1:2–3. In a courtroom picture, God called on the earth and all of its peoples to witness the charges he brought against both Israel and Judah and the judgment he pronounced. God was coming down from his exalted place in the heavens to bring judgment.

1:4–5. The punishment is pictured as a catastrophic divine visitation. The poetic imagery is rich in its description. Mountains melt and valleys burst open and become like melted wax at the presence of God. What chance, then, does a mere human being have in the time of God's visitation? Except in the merciful forgiveness of God, people cannot stand before God. Both Israel and Judah are pictured as unrepentant sinner nations facing the wrath of a righteous God.

Micah identified the sins of the two nations with their capital cities, Samaria and Jerusalem. The "high place [or places] of Judah" refers to the places where the pagan religious practices of the people were carried out, usually on the hilltops where the Baal and Asherah shrines were located. This demoralizing worship usually involved religious prostitutes.

1:6–7. Samaria was the focus of this judgment oracle. Note the description of the ruined city: a heap in the country, planted with vineyards, the foundations of her great buildings no more than rubble fallen into the valley. If you go to the site of ancient Samaria today, this is an apt description of what you will see. Of course, the images of Baal and Asherah are gone. Such images and other adornments made of precious metals were purchased by the gifts or fees paid to the religious prostitutes, and all these would be gone. God's righteous judgment would bring to an end the wicked city.

Mourning Samaria, Warning Jerusalem (1:8–9)

Micah mourned the destruction of Samaria that he had witnessed. He warned of a similar fate for Jerusalem. "For this" likely indicates that Micah had seen the devastation of Samaria. The picture following is one of mourning, the great sadness expressed at the tragedy. Nakedness refers to going without the outer garments, wearing only a loincloth. The cry of the jackal, a scavenging animal, would come as the jackal sought the human and animal remains in the ruins of the city. The sound of the ostrich was mournful. As the prophet mourned the destruction of Samaria, he warned that the same fate threatened Jerusalem.

Sounding the Alarm in the Cities of Judah (1:10–16)

Translating this passage into English (or any other language) cannot preserve the force and meaning. Here is a series of literary puns, in which a key word in a statement is followed by another sounding much like the first. These cities of Judah were in the plain between Jerusalem and the coast. This area was Micah's home. Each city was warned of impending disaster, including his home town. The inhabitants were told to shave their heads, a sign of mourning, as they anticipated the carrying away of their children to slavery.

Do Not Covet (2:1–9)

2:1. A basic law at the foundation of Hebrew society was being flagrantly broken by the powerful and heartless men of Judah. A study of the laws given in the Old Testament reveals that violations deliberately done were more serious than those thoughtlessly done. Micah spoke here of the hardened, deliberate breaking of God's commandments. After tossing through the night as these powerful men devised their evil plans to increase their wealth, at dawn they moved to carry out the plans made in their nighttime plotting. They succeeded in their wicked plans, not because the plans were legal or just, but simply because these men had the power to carry them out. It is the story of the powerful versus the powerless. They lived by their own rule: might makes right.

2:2. Land grabbing was clearly a problem. Amos condemned it (Amos 2:7; 8:4) as did Isaiah (Isaiah 5:8–10). Land is valuable in any society and in any country, but nowhere more than in Palestine. The background of the Hebrews from the time of Abraham through their days in the wilderness with Moses was that of wanderers—either bedouin nomads or semi-nomads. Except for their days in Egypt, most of it as slaves, the Hebrews wandered with flocks and herds. But once they came into Canaan and possessed fertile land where they could produce food and live all year in the same place, they highly treasured their land.

The laws the Hebrews were given testify to the importance of land. Land was to be treasured and cared for. Every seventh year the land was to lie fallow, unplanted, so it could regain its strength or fertility (Exodus 23:10–11). Once the Hebrew farmer lost his land, slavery was the assured result for him and his family. Joshua 14—21 gives in great detail how the land in Canaan was apportioned fairly to the various tribes. Leviticus 25 sets out specific laws governing land: its use, sale, and purchase. Among the Hebrews land could be "sold," but on the fiftieth year, called the Year of Jubilee, all land would revert to its original owner or his heirs. In reality, land could only be leased for the years remaining until the Year of Jubilee. These rules applied only to land outside walled cities. Property inside walled cities fell under different rules. Property there could be sold, subject only to redemption by a kinsman within one year after its original sale. If no kinsman claimed it and paid the sale price within one year, the property was assigned permanently to the new owner.

The focus of what Micah said was not to remind those of his day of the details of what their law said. His concern was to address their greed and covetous grasping for land not theirs. Coveting was forbidden the Hebrews in their basic laws—the Ten Commandments given as primary laws in their covenant relationship with Yahweh. "You shall not covet your neighbor's house; you shall not covet your neighbor's wife, or male or female slave, or ox, or donkey, or anything that belongs to your neighbor" (Ex. 20:17). To covet means to have an intense desire or lust for something or someone. This final commandment is the one looking inside the mind and heart. It deals less with action than with the attitude that leads to breaking or keeping other commandments. If our inner thought and attitude is right before God, then our action will follow in the right ways.

Micah here saw a very wrong attitude in powerful men among his people. They not only had the intense, lustful desire to possess their neighbors' lands. They also had the power to take, illegal though it was, their neighbors' lands that they coveted. Isaiah painted a picture of the land-grabbing wealthy of this time (Isa. 5:8). He described the one who had taken field after field and house after house, until finally he lived absolutely alone in the middle of the land!

2:3–4. What was in store for these greedy men? God had a plan to deal with them. They would walk no more with a haughty, prideful attitude. Their power and wealth had served to keep away any deserved punishment. Now they could escape no longer. They would be sinners in the hands of a righteous God. As these once powerful ones were shamed by the "taunt song," they would moan about their losses, complaining that God had changed the "inheritance," taking away the Promised Land they had received. Now this land was in the hands of their captors. How easy it was for them to blame God for any misfortune that came. Now the Assyrians would distribute the land.

2:5. These once powerful men would have "no one to cast the line by lot in the assembly of the LORD." Previously these men had enjoyed great influence in decisions concerning the land—decisions properly made by casting the sacred lots but likely controlled by their bribes. Now their ill-gotten land would be divided among the poor by their Assyrian conquerors.

2:6. Stung by his message, a "prophet" in tune with these powerful, wealthy men interrupted Micah with a self-justifying response of denial. *Why, they want to know, would you preach such a message? You should never say such things. Such disgraces will never happen to us.*

2:7. Micah kept to his message of warning from God. He responded with four questions addressed to the people of Israel, not just to these he condemned. (1) "Should this be said?" He in effect asked the people, not just the wealthy, *Have I not told the truth about what has been done?* (2) "Is the LORD's patience exhausted?" This suggests that even God's patience with sinners eventually runs out. (3) "Are these his doings?" The question focuses on whether the deeds of these powerful oppressors were in keeping with the will and law of God. Obviously not! (4) "Do not my words do good to one who walks uprightly?" There had been no message of condemnation to the one whose deeds were in keeping with the will and law of God.

2:8–9. In case there was any doubt about the guilt of those condemned, Micah again cataloged some of their oppressive actions against the poor and powerless. The common people were treated like an enemy. The unsuspecting peaceful were stripped of even their personal possessions. Widows and children were driven out of their homes. Their only option as homeless ones would be slavery. The phrase, "you take away my glory forever," probably referred to the loss of a future generation of God-fearing citizens to be the core of the citizens of the land.

Focusing on the Meaning

Covetousness—greedy desire for what someone else has and you do not have—is as much a problem today as it was in Micah's, and perhaps even more today, because there are more "things" to covet. Covetousness is rooted in an attitude of selfishness. When this selfish greed is joined with power, it becomes like a raging wildfire, consuming everything in sight.

In many ways the eighth century BC, the time of Amos, Hosea, and Micah, was much like today. There is prosperity, but there are the poor and disadvantaged. God did not oppose the rich for being rich, but he warned of the danger of wanting more and more.

Power comes with wealth, and that is one of the places where the message of Micah speaks to our age. Instead of using that power to increase wealth at the expense of the poor, we must expend power and wealth to better the circumstances of the poor.

Covetousness for more things can lead to the neglect and ultimate decay of family life and the home. Loving care for and time spent with children in the home will, in the long run, count for much more than making the children the best dressed in the community. Taking time to be in church with them will expose children to the eternal values that are more precious than any earthly treasure. We must remember that Christianity is always just one generation away from extinction. If we are not faithful in teaching our children about God we may be fulfilling the warning of Micah 2:9b, and from our young children we may take away God's glory forever.

The people of Micah's day wanted to hear preaching about other things. The message of Micah made them too uncomfortable because of their guilt. A true message from God's word will point out to us our personal needs. If we feel it addresses only other people, we need some critical self-examination.

Measure your desire for more things in your life and the time you expend on getting them against the desire you have for spiritual growth and the time you expend in that quest. Covetousness is not really about having material things but about the priority they take in your life.

TEACHING PLANS

Teaching Plans—Varied Learning Activities

Connect with Life

1. Prior to class, find pictures of things in the world that might cause people to covet. (Pictures of expensive cars, homes, attractive men/women, and material things can easily be found in magazines or newspapers.) Create a collage of these images and have it displayed when members arrive.

2. Enlist a class member to read the Main Idea for this lesson from the *Study Guide*: "God judges people who oppress others in their desire to have more things for themselves." Ask members what they think about this statement, and then encourage them to find the motivation behind the examples in the "Coveting Collage" (see step 1).

3. Tell the class that today we are going to focus on the Question to Explore: "What place does the desire for things have in my life?" Lead in prayer, asking God to reveal the answer during the lesson time.

Guide Bible Study

4. Write on the board:

   • The Judge
   • The Plaintiff (the aggrieved party)
   • The Defendant

   Divide the class into three groups, assigning each group one of the participants. Explain to the class that the Scriptures being read are like an account of a legal proceeding. Encourage class members to read the Focal Text with this idea in mind. Have two class members read Micah 1:1–7 and 2:1–9 aloud.

5. Ask the group who focused on "The Defendant" to report their findings. Ask, *Who is the defendant in this case?* Have class members

give Scripture references with their answers. (Possible answers include Judah, Samaria, all the people of earth, Jacob, Israel, etc.)

6. Ask the group who focused on "The Plaintiff" to report their findings. Encourage the group to discuss what the Scripture passages indicate about how God is caused pain. Ask, *Who is it that God is accusing of having caused this pain, or having committed sin?* (Samaria, Judah, especially the rich and powerful)

7. Using the information in the *Study Guide*, explain to the class the meaning of the term "witness" (1:2). Ask, *What implications does this have in light of the people of the earth being called before God? What might God say about us if God were to witness against us today?*

8. Ask, *What sin(s) had been committed?* List responses on the board. Possible answers include:

   • Prostitution/idolatry (1:7)
   • Planning to do harm to others (2:1)
   • Desiring others' lands and possessions (2:2)
   • Evil behavior towards one another (2:8—9)

9. Ask the group who focused on "The Judge" to report. Have the group list from the Scripture passages God's actions towards those who had committed these sins. (Possible answers include: planning disaster, 2:3; bringing ridicule to the people, 2:4; and having their land taken and divided from among them (2:4b).

Encourage Application

10. Note that Micah's message was to convey God's displeasure with the people's covetousness. Ask, *Who is it that is really hurt when people covet? What is the effect on a person's family when a person covets? Does coveting ever hurt in such a way that it is impossible to repair?*

11. Have someone read aloud Micah 2:1. Ask, *Is it permissible to do something simply because we have the ability? Does coveting something necessarily lead to sin? Is there any harm in desiring better facilities for the church buildings, or more members for the choir, or a greater budget?*

12. Read the following illustration and have learners respond to it using the provided questions: A person was using his computer and

decided to get on the internet. As he was surfing, he kept getting these pop-up web advertisements that were for online casinos. He decided to check one out, and found out that it was extremely easy to play. He ended up playing computer Blackjack, and he won $20.00! Ask, *Was playing these computer casino games a form of coveting? What harm might come from this activity? Who might get hurt from this activity?*

13.   Use the questions in the *Study Guide* to guide a discussion of coveting.

Teaching Plan—Lecture and Questions

Connect with Life

1. Inform class members that the next four weeks will be a study of what God requires from us as Christians in today's society. Specify that today's lesson is about coveting and the effects it can have on the body of Christ.

2. Give a brief summary of the setting for the Book of Micah, using the information on Micah 1:1 in the *Study Guide*. If available, display a map with the land of Israel shown in Micah's time.

Guide Bible Study

3.   Read Micah 1:2–4 aloud. Ask class members to give adjectives that describe God's coming judgment. (Possible answers might include: powerful, 2:4; and personal, 2:3).

4. Ask, *Why was God bringing judgment and speaking against the nation?* Refer to the *Study Guide* for information regarding the word "witness" and share it with the class.

5. Invite members to read Micah 1:5–7 to themselves. Comment on why God was angry with the people of Samaria. (Note that this proclamation against the people is different from the proclamation against Judah found in Micah 2.) (Possible answers might include idolatry, unfaithfulness, etc.)

6. Summarize briefly 1:8–16, using information in the *Study Guide*

and in "Bible Comments" in this *Teaching Guide.*

7. Invite someone to read aloud the Main Idea for this lesson: "God judges people who oppress others in their desire to have more things for themselves." Invite members to comment on this statement. Then read aloud Micah 2:1–2 and encourage the class to summarize the charge in their own words.

8. Using the *Study Guide*, explain the meaning of the word "power" (2:1). Ask, *If something is within our power to accomplish, does that mean that we should do it?*

9. Read aloud 2:3–4. Invite the class to comment on the actions of the people. Briefly mention from the *Study Guide* the importance of property to the Hebrews. Lead members to give examples of how this type of coveting might be encountered today.

10. Invite members to read 2:3-5 to discover how God would respond to the people's sin. Write the answers on the board. (Possible answers might include: God would destroy their land; God would bring them shame; God would allow their enemies to rule them.)

Encourage Application

11. Remark that being a Christian in today's society means that we sometimes will have to forgo things that others might have. Ask, *What might happen to our lives if we coveted, as did the people in Micah's time?*

12. Ask, *What is one way we can keep from coveting things in our lives?* Read aloud the third stanza of the hymn, "Count Your Blessings."[1] Have members respond to this suggestion.

13. Encourage members to evaluate their lives to find areas in which to improve their control over desires that could lead to coveting. Close the lesson by asking God to reveal these areas to us and to help us overcome the temptation to covet.

NOTES

1. "Count Your Blessings," words by Johnson Oatman, Jr., 1897.

Focal Text

Micah 3

Background

Micah 3

Main Idea

God holds leaders accountable for behaving justly and leading people in the right way.

Question to Explore

What leadership qualities do you value?

Teaching Aim

To lead participants to decide to exercise the leadership traits God blesses and encourage these traits in leaders they support

MICAH

What the Lord Requires

Lesson Twelve

When Leaders Sell Out

BIBLE COMMENTS

Understanding the Context

A land under the pressures of an outside enemy force of significantly great power desperately needs strong and effective leadership. That the nation of Judah faced a crisis of major dimension in the lifetime of Micah is without question. Assyria was mighty and powerful, with aggressive goals and a military force fully capable of carrying out its goals. Their military might is sometimes compared to the later Roman army—well-trained, dedicated, capable, almost invincible. Their boasting of their might and cruelty to any who fought against them caused enemies and potential enemies to shudder with fear.

Mightier than all the forces of Assyria was the Lord of Hosts. If Israel or Judah was to meet the Assyrians successfully, they would prevail through the power of their God rather than their military might. False leaders would fuel false hopes and lead the nation to disaster. The leadership of the house of Israel seemed to be more concerned with the growth of their personal wealth than they were with the direction and fate of the nation. Their deeds were guided more by covetous desires than by a true and serious commitment to Yahweh.

Sadly, the religious leaders, the priests and prophets, were a sorry lot as well. They were interested more in gain than in godly truth. Covetousness was rampant and the moving force of the day. In such a dearth of true prophecy as well as moral and political leadership, the prophet stepped out with a message from God for this wayward and rebellious people.

Interpreting the Scriptures

False Political Leaders (3:1–4)

3:1–2. Micah addressed the heads of Jacob and rulers of the house of Israel. These were the civil or political leaders of the nation. The "heads of Jacob" and "rulers of the house of Israel" refer to the same leaders. One of the common features of Hebrew poetry is called parallelism, which simply means that consecutive statements carry the same thought or meaning. Remember that Jacob was renamed Israel after he met and wrestled with the angel of Yahweh (Genesis 32:28).

Leaders of the nation should know justice—that which is right according to God's law and teaching. But, no! Instead they "hate the good and love the evil." "Good," as it is used in the Old Testament, simply means what is pleasing to God, what is in accord with God's will. The key to understanding the Old Testament meaning of this word is found in Genesis 1:3–4. After God had said, "Let there be light," God looked at the light and said it was "good." He did not attribute to the light a morally upright quality. He simply affirmed that it was exactly what he had called for. It conformed totally to his will.

"Evil" is the opposite of "good." So evil, as it is used in the Old Testament, describes anything that does not please God, or that which does not conform to God's will. How much worse can leaders be if they hate what pleases God and love what does not please God?

3:3–4. How do these leaders, these "heads" and "rulers," treat their subjects? Like a butcher treats a wild animal. They tear the skin off them. As we might say, they "skin them alive." Then they break their bones and chop up the flesh to cook in the kettle and eat it. Again the figures show leaders who are interested in their personal gain with no concern for those they are supposed to lead.

After such treatment of their subjects they cry to Yahweh. They obviously are only pretending when they claim Yahweh as their God. Instead of answering their cries, God would hide his face from them. Their deeds were contrary to what God wished.

The False Prophets (3:5-7)

In this passage three different words are used for the prophets. The most often used word for prophet in the Old Testament appears in 3:5-6. The word *nabi'*, usually translated "prophet," refers to one who is a spokesperson for God. He or she delivers a message received from God. It can best be explained by looking at Exodus 7:1. Here, after Moses claimed he was not a good speaker, God sent his brother, Aaron, to speak for him to Pharaoh: "The LORD said to Moses, 'See, I have made you like God to Pharaoh, and your brother Aaron shall be your prophet [*nabi'*].'"

How does the prophet come to know the message of God? The passage in the Bible that speaks most clearly to this is in Jeremiah 23, especially verses 16-22. The true prophet is taken into the "council of the Lord" (Jer. 23:18). There he can both see and hear the word that the Lord has for him to deliver to the people. Concerning the false prophet, the message from the Lord through Jeremiah was: "I did not send the prophets, yet they ran; I did not speak to them, yet they prophesied. But if they had stood in my council then they would have proclaimed my words to my people . . ." (Jer. 23:21-22).

The second word used for "prophet" appears in the first line of verse 7: "seers." The primary meaning is *to see.* The emphasis is on the ability of the person to see beyond normal sight. The word usually refers to a true prophet.

The third word, used in the next line of verse 7, is "diviners," which refers to a soothsayer or one practicing witchcraft. It probably refers to those who had been banned from the land (see Deuteronomy 18:10-11).

False prophets were a plague to true prophets. Their messages were always more pleasing to the hearers. For example, Jeremiah had a sad duty—to urge the citizens of Jerusalem to surrender to Babylon in the face of certain conquest and destruction of the city. He did so using the visual aid of wearing an ox yoke, urging the people to submit to the yoke of Babylon. It was the punishment they must suffer. But Hananiah, who we know was a false prophet, followed him and his message by smashing the ox yoke in the streets of the city, declaring that so God would destroy the yoke of the Babylonians (see Jer. 27—28). Hananiah's message was much more desirable than Jeremiah's. Sometimes the false prophets were seeking public honor and acclaim. Perhaps even more often they were seeking material or financial rewards. Micah faced greedy false prophets.

Using all three of the Hebrew terms for "prophet," Micah denounced the false prophets of his day. The major problem Micah addressed in these false prophets was that of selfish greed. Pay the prophet well and you will get a word of wholeness, or peace (*shalom*). But if you do not, war is declared against you. The authentic word of God was of no value; only personal material gain was important to these false prophets.

See the graphic picture drawn in 3:6. For those who claimed to be able to see what others could not, there would be darkness and night, no sun and a black day. To those who claimed to have visionary insight and abilities there would be no vision and no revelation. Seers and diviners would have no answers to give and would be disgraced.

The True Prophet (3:8)

In contrast to the false prophets who were concerned only with material gain from their "prophetic" words, Micah described the true prophet— one filled with power and the Spirit of the Lord. This was what separated the true from the false. True, it was not always easy for the hearers to distinguish the true from the false, and many of the Hebrews were misled. The message of the true prophet was different from that of the false prophet. The true prophet pointed out the transgressions and sins of the nation. For this unpopular message no one would *put something into his mouth* (3:5).

The Nation's Corrupt Leadership (3:9–11)

The leaders of the nation were acting unjustly and corruptly. They not only failed to practice justice, or right action, but also they abhorred it. They regarded justice as an abomination. Justice was something they tried to keep away from. "All that is straight they have made crooked" is a literal translation of the Hebrew, which the NRSV renders as "pervert all equity" (3:9).

Jerusalem was being built with blood and unrighteousness. All of the leaders—rulers, priests, and prophets—were looking for bribes but at the same time mouthing words of false religious faith: "Surely the LORD is with us; no harm shall come upon us" (3:11).

The leadership of the nation, civil and religious, was morally, ethically, and religiously bankrupt. It was all a sham.

Jerusalem Is Doomed! (3:12)

Zion will become a plowed field? Jerusalem a heap of ruins? Is that what we heard? So the citizens who heard Micah's message must have said. *Unthinkable!*

But Micah had their attention at last. This message probably made more of an impression on his contemporaries than any other he spoke. About a century later, Jeremiah, the prophet, was speaking a similar message predicting doom and destruction for Jerusalem and the temple. Jeremiah's message was that Yahweh would "make this house [the temple] like Shiloh and I will make this city a curse for all the nations of the earth" (Jer. 26:6).

The reference to Shiloh is to 1 Samuel 4, where the Philistines captured the ark of the covenant in the battle of Aphek-Ebenezer. They then pursued the Hebrew army to Shiloh, where the tabernacle (then serving as the temple) was located. They then completely destroyed it.

Jeremiah was arrested and put on trial for his life for having spoken of the destruction of the temple and Jerusalem. Jeremiah was freed of the charge because almost a century earlier, Micah had made a similar prophecy that King Hezekiah had believed. Hezekiah had repented, entreating the favor of the Lord, and the Lord had changed his mind about the disaster that the prophet had predicted (Jer. 26:18–19).

The story of Hezekiah's repentance and the part the prophet Isaiah played in these events is recorded in 2 Kings 19:14–37. Micah is not mentioned in the account in Kings, but the accounts in Micah and especially in Jeremiah fill in the part he played in these significant events.

Focusing on the Meaning

Leaders can make all the difference in the world. Micah describes a situation in which weak and godless leaders were leading the nation on a collision course with disaster. When the true prophets finally got the ear of King Hezekiah, the course of the nation changed drastically. True, Hezekiah was only one man; but in a leadership role he was able to save the nation from disaster. In the United States we have the privilege and responsibility of choosing our leaders. A serious obligation is laid on us as Christians both to serve as leaders and to participate in the process of choosing the right kind of leaders.

The leaders Micah spoke about in this lesson operated on the *what's-in-it-for-me* standard. Those who operate on that standard do not deserve the title of leader. The true leader who is worth the title will ask instead, *What can I do to make this place, organization, company, church, community, etc., better and more effective and make the lives it touches happier, better, and more productive of what is good for all of us?* "Servant leadership" is a term often used today and is appropriate for those who aspire to leadership positions. I have never seen a church that could not benefit from more committed leadership from among its members.

The Hebrews of Jerusalem and Judah in Micah's time felt secure, believing that God would protect them. *After all,* they must have reasoned, *God has been our God and we have been his people at least ever since the time of Moses—at least for the past 500 years. God knows that; we know that. Don't worry; God will care for us.* And that must have been the extent of the religious devotion of many if not most of the people. But it was not enough. Are we in danger of falling into the same trap? We claim that we are a Christian nation. We get upset when someone tries to remove "under God" from our pledge to the flag. But how many of us worship regularly? And how many who do worship provide committed Christian leadership in our communities?

In the days of Micah, Jerusalem was not destroyed. Why? Because God used his prophet leaders to call the king and others to repentance, and there was genuine repentance. God had decreed destruction. Repentance enabled God to withhold the punishment.

We need to remember that God is always looking for a chance to withhold the devastating judgment people's rebellion requires from a just and righteous God. In the presence of sin, repentance is always needed.

TEACHING PLANS

Teaching Plans—Varied Learning Activities

Connect with Life

1. Write on the board: *Follow the Leader?* Ask, *What qualities must leaders have for people to follow them?* Write responses on the board.

2. Ask members to give examples of leaders who have influenced a large group of people. Write their names on the board. Compare the names of the leaders given to the list of qualities on the board. Ask, *Which of these qualities do you think God would most want a leader to have?*

3. Have someone read aloud the Main Idea for this lesson: "God holds leaders accountable for behaving justly and leading people in the right way." Explain to the class the meaning of leaders being accountable.

Guide Bible Study

4. Briefly review the last portion of Micah 2, reminding class members that God was bringing judgment on Judah for their sin of coveting. Have someone read aloud Micah 3:1–2a. Ask, *To whom was Micah referring? Was his audience in the beginning of chapter 3 the same or different from his audience in Chapter 2?* (different)

5. Note that Micah was making a plea to those who were responsible for leading the people of Judah. Using the *Study Guide*, explain the word "know" in 3:2. Have someone read aloud Genesis 4:1, and then ask, *What was Micah saying about the spiritual state of the leaders?* (Lead members to discover that the leaders were more intimate with their own desires than with the will of God.)

6. Enlist someone to read Micah 3:2b–3 aloud. Invite members to comment on the verses. Use the comments in the *Study Guide* and in "Bible Comments" in this *Teaching Guide* to explain the verses. Ask, *Do Christians ever treat one another as carelessly as this?*

7. Encourage members to respond to verse 4. Ask, *What are some things that Christians might do that would cause God to "hide his face from them"?* Compare these answers with the list of leadership qualities on the board.

8. Have class members form these two groups:
   • Prophets
   • Government/Civic Leaders

   Read Micah 3:5–12 aloud, and encourage members to listen for actions that were committed that show evidence of ungodly behavior.

Then have groups find consequences of these actions within these verses.

9. Have the "Prophet" group report, sharing the actions that were condemned by God. Explain the phrase "lead . . . astray" (3:5) using comments from the *Study Guide*. Ask, *In what ways do these actions grieve God?*

10. Have the "Government/Civic Leaders" group report. Ask, *In whom or what were these leaders placing their trust?* Next, inquire, *How would this affect the people?* Note that these leaders were motivated by the desire to have monetary gain. Ask, *Do churches ever behave in this way, allowing desire for money to become their motivation?*

11. Read Micah 3:8 aloud, and explain that Micah was showing himself to be accountable to God, separating himself from the other prophets because of God's presence in his life. Have both groups evaluate their subjects and determine to whom the prophets or civic leaders were accountable. Have both groups list one or two ideas that might help leaders in such roles today become more accountable to their respective constituents.

Encourage Application

12. Note that even though the message was given to both religious and civic leaders, it was given to the religious leaders first. Ask, *What does this imply to the religious leaders we support?*

13. Ask the following questions, allowing time to respond:

    • What are some indications that a Christian might have unhealthy attitudes about wealth?
    • What are some indications that a church might have unhealthy attitudes about wealth?
    • Is it acceptable for a church to base its health on attendance figures and budget numbers? To whom is the church accountable?
    • How appropriate is it for a pastoral leader within a church to behave like a CEO in a large corporation? To whom would a leader like this be accountable?
    • How can we learn to exercise the leadership traits God blesses?
    • How can we encourage these traits in leaders we support?

14. Close in prayer, asking the Holy Spirit to fill members' lives (and yours) with attributes that are godly and holy, so that God's style of leadership creates yours.

Teaching Plan—Lecture and Questions

Connect with Life

1. Prior to the arrival of members, list on the board several influential figures in history. Write this question on the board: *What makes a leader a leader?*

2. Read aloud the Main Idea for this lesson, informing class members that leaders are accountable not only to those whom they lead, but first and foremost, to God. Tell the account of Howard Thurmond's grandmother to the class.

3. Lead the class in a prayer (or have someone else pray), asking God to help members exercise the leadership traits God blesses and encourage these traits in leaders they support.

Guide Bible Study

4. Ask, *What was Micah rebuking the nation for in the last chapter?* (The people were guilty of covetousness.) Point out that in this lesson, Micah continued to witness against the people. Specifically, Micah was rebuking the leaders of Judah, both the religious and civic/governmental leaders. Read Micah 3:1–4 aloud.

5. Note to the class the wrongs Micah addressed in the leaders:

   • Lovers of evil/haters of good (3:2)
   • Cannibals (3:4)

   Explain to the class the words "love" and "hate," as described in the *Study Guide* and in "Bible Comments" in this *Teaching Guide*. Refer to the example of Thurmond's grandmother, and ask, *Was the preacher looking out for the "common good" of the people or more concerned with himself?*

6. Read aloud 3:5–8. Lead class members to find the differences between the messages of the false prophets and Micah. Ask, *Why were the false prophets promising peace when Micah was promising God's judgment?*

7. Using the *Study Guide*, explain to the class the punishments given to the prophets, seers, and diviners in 3:6–7. Contrast these punishments with Micah's explanation of his life in 3:8.

8. Read aloud 3:9–12, asking members to listen for the sins of the governmental leaders. Ask, *How were the civic and government leaders bringing judgment on themselves?* Compare their attitudes with the attitudes of the prophets in 3:5–8. Ask, *What was the common denominator in the attitudes of these two groups?* (Greed)

9. Read verse 11 aloud and explain the attitudes of the leaders. Ask, *How could the leaders feel that no harm could come to them?*

Encourage Application

10. Summarize the lesson, being certain to explain the necessity for accountability to God as leaders. Ask, *If you were praying that the Holy Spirit would fill your life with a certain attribute, what might it be?*

11. Ask, *What are five attributes that a Christian leader could have that would be unhealthy? What are some possible indicators that a church has an unhealthy attitude towards wealth?*

12. Read the "Case Study" from the *Study Guide*. Ask the questions at the end of the study, and give time for class members to respond.

13. Close with prayer, thanking God for leadership worthy to be followed.

Focal Text
Micah 4:1–8; 5:2–5a

Background
Micah 4—5

Main Idea
God will provide peace to people who respond in faithfulness to him.

Question to Explore
Is peace really possible?

Teaching Aim
To lead adults to describe the peace God provides and commit themselves to live in faithfulness to God

MICAH

What the Lord Requires

Lesson Thirteen

Peace Is Coming

BIBLE COMMENTS

Understanding the Context

Beyond the disaster and doom pictured in the earlier chapters, Micah turned to a message of hope and assurance. No specific timelines were set forth; it was sufficient to affirm the purpose of the Lord to accomplish good things with and through his people. Bible scholars disagree on how to understand and apply many of the statements in these two chapters. It is impossible to speak with certainty about the chronology involved and the specific application of various statements. It is important that we remember that we have as guides for understanding these and other words all the rest of the Scriptures and the Spirit God has granted to lead us.

God is a God of peace. Those who would describe the God of the Old Testament as a harsh, frightful, warlike God whose messengers were regularly sent with a message of doom, doom, doom, have missed the point. His desire for people and the world was and is peace.

The Hebrew word for peace is both beautiful and filled with meaning. The word is *shalom*. It is usually simply translated as "peace." It means much more than just the cessation or absence of hostilities. It indicates a wholeness or completeness in a positive relationship. When we have

136

peace with God, the barriers created by our rebellion against God are all broken and thrown far away. Without fear or hesitation we can come to God, much as a disobedient child who has been forgiven his misdeeds can jump into the outstretched arms of a loving human father or mother.

We think that we know and practice love. Try to imagine what it took for a father to send his son to face what Jesus faced—and that out of love for you and me and all the rest of the human race. That includes the murderers, rapists, terrorists, and all the others who commit even the most horrendous deeds. That took a love beyond that of which we are humanly capable. Such love is found only with God. The God of the Old Testament is also the God of the New Testament. He is unchanged and unchanging.

When we turn the page to Micah 4, we do not meet another God. Rather we see more of the same God, who still sits in judgment on sin, but who loves and wants to forgive and restore the sinner. Humankind is basically the same as in the time in which Micah lived; neither has God changed. We begin to see the *why* of the messages of doom and judgment—so that God can bring humanity into peace—*shalom*—wholeness, to become what God intended people to be from the start.

Interpreting the Scriptures

Some readers are puzzled by the fact that Micah 4:1–3 is almost word for word the same as Isaiah 4:2–4. No one knows whether Micah copied Isaiah, Isaiah copied Micah, or whether both used a poem penned by another writer. The last seems more likely, although no one knows. We can rest assured that whoever the human writer may have been, this message originated with the God who inspired both the writing and the inclusion of these words in both books.

God's Plan for the Future of Jerusalem and for a Rebuilt Temple (4:1–2)

4:1. "In days to come" is sometimes translated "in the last days" (NIV, NASB). It may also be translated "in latter days." It does not refer to the end of time but to some future time without giving a specific date. Remember that the immediately preceding passage speaks of the coming destruction of Jerusalem and the temple. Also remember that chapter and verse markers or breaks were not a part of the original text of the Bible.

They were added centuries after the time of Micah. Micah must be speaking of the promised restoration of the nation after what we today call the Exile. He had just spoken of the destruction of the Jerusalem temple. Here he affirmed the promise of restoration and the hope for a glorious day. In stirring poetic imagery he described the impressive glory of the rebuilt temple in terms of a mountain raised high above all surrounding ones to draw the attention of all who may see it.

4:2. This exalted rebuilt temple would serve not only the Hebrews, but many nations. The hope of the future, according to Micah, would not be in the sacrifices to be offered there, but in the instruction in God's ways that would be available there. Instruction in the word of the Lord is the hope of humankind. Micah did not rule out or speak against the sacrifices used in their religion, but teaching and learning the ways of God would become primary. A part of the duty of the priest in ancient Israel was to lead the people in obeying all of the Law, the *torah* (the first five books of the Bible). A careful reading of the Old Testament suggests that the temple and the priests had centered their work on sacrifices and worship related to these sacrifices. Now the focus would change to teaching God's word to enable the worshipers to walk in God's paths. The Hebrew word translated "walk" often means not *to stroll down a pathway*, but *to live a life*. If the people were to be God's people and fulfill what God had called them to be, they must live the lives to which God called them and become "a blessing to all the families [nations] of the earth" (Genesis 12:3).

A Resulting Era of Peace (4:3–5)

4:3. This verse indicates the marks of a time of peace. This peaceful time would have true justice. God himself would be the judge, and there would be absolute fairness in God's decisions between the nations. Disarmament is a dream of peacemakers in our age, but it would be a reality in Micah's time of peace. The focus would be on food aplenty for the needs of humankind. The swords and spears would be beaten out into plowshares and pruning instruments. The instruments of war would become the tools with which to feed the poor and hungry. Nations would be at peace so much so that there would be no need to train armies any more.

4:4. Security and happiness are the elements of the picture painted by these words. Each family would have its home with productive fig bushes and grape vines growing to shade the yard. In this quiet security, people would live in the abundance pictured. There would be no cause for fear. This is the promise of God himself.

4:5. Other nations may have their gods, but this age of peace comes as we "walk" or *live our lives* in the name of Yahweh our God. Remember that the Hebrews had nothing physical of their God except his name (Exodus 3:13–15). This faithfulness to God must not be temporary, but forever and forever. How long is forever? The Hebrew word *'olam* which we usually translate *forever* or *eternity* means *as far as you can see and then on to the unseen future with no imaginable end.* It is impossible for our finite minds to comprehend the extent of *'olam—eternity.*

The Restoration of the Nation (4:6–8)

These verses picture a restored nation, strong and well-established, to be ruled from Jerusalem. God is capable of taking the lame, the homeless, and the afflicted, and molding them into a great nation. That is because God will be ruling them. How long? As long as God is ruling it will be forever—to *'olam.*

The Suffering and Triumph of the Nation (4:9—5:1)

This passage, although not a part of our focal text, requires a few words of explanation. In poetic form it speaks of the defeat and destruction experienced by Jerusalem and the kingdom of Judah. The citizens, at least many of them, were exiled to Babylon. These events occurred in 587 BC. From this exile they and their descendants were rescued beginning in 539 BC, when the first deportees were permitted to return and begin rebuilding their lives in Jerusalem and Judah.

Discussions abound about these words. Some contend that these were predictions from Micah in the eighth century BC concerning events to happen in the sixth century BC and the years thereafter. Others reason that these words must come from a later prophet and were added to Micah's message to explain how matters turned out for the nation. No matter which you may choose, the message came from God and affirms God's work in and control of the fortunes of the nations—especially of those who serve God.

A stark contrast is painted between what is now and what is to be for the nation. "Now" appears three times in this passage, in 4:9; 4:11; and 5:1. Each depicts the imminent troubles to face Judah. Each is followed by a message of hope and deliverance. The hope message following the third of these is the oracle about the king from Bethlehem, discussed in the following section.

The Promise of a New Ruler from Bethlehem (5:2–5a)

This, perhaps the best-known passage in Micah, tells of the king from Bethlehem who would lead his people to a time of security and peace. We are tempted to see this passage only in the light of its use in Matthew, but we also need to see what it said and meant to the contemporaries of Micah in the eighth century BC. Bethlehem (an older name for the town or area of Bethlehem was Ephrathah) was a small and insignificant town. It was only four or five miles south of Jerusalem. Its small population was dependent on sheep herding for a livelihood. It was the home of the clan of Jesse, the father of David.

David's accomplishments and his reputation marked him as the ideal king. He was a charismatic leader who had united the nation and led it to its greatest glory. His leadership was not only in the political and secular affairs, but even more so in the realm of religious and spiritual devotion. Of course, every king who ruled the kingdom of Judah was a descendant of David. But they all, especially those who followed David's son, Solomon, fell far short of the example David had set.

Those who heard Micah in his day belonged to a small and powerless nation, threatened by the mighty and dominating Assyrian empire. Micah's message envisioned a new king from the line of David who would, as David had, lead them to a time of peace and security and to sincere religious devotion to their God.

The ultimate fulfillment of these words was not to come for centuries, when one of the line of David was born in Bethlehem, his birth heralded by the songs of angels (see Matthew 2:1–6; Luke 2:1–20). One of the marvelous features of the prophetic messages is that they have meaning to those who initially heard them as well as meanings, usually fuller and greater, to future generations. This passage was a message of hope and of God's purpose to care for his people in Micah's time. Yet Matthew and other New Testament writers saw it speaking to and completed or fulfilled in the days of the Messiah in which they were privileged to live. Hopefully we can see it today as applicable to our lives as well. We can know the Promised One who came and can experience the eternal peace that comes from knowing him.

The themes in this message center in the hope that God cares for his creation, his people. Note especially the characteristics of the rule of this promised one. He would sustain them, feeding them in the strength and majesty of God himself, leading them to security because all will recognize his greatness and his devotion to peace.

This passage is quoted in Matthew 2:5–6. To the palace of Herod the king in Jerusalem had come the magi or wise men from the east. They were seeking the new king whose birth had been heralded by the star they had followed. The scholars Herod consulted pointed to this passage, sending the seeking travelers to Bethlehem, where they found the Christ child.

Focusing on the Meaning

God is a God of peace, and God calls his followers to honor, practice, and work for peace. Those who claim to be his people populate large sections of the earth and are counted as the most numerous religious group among the people of our planet. Yet wars have not disappeared. Perhaps wars have diminished in number, but they have become more deadly as the technology of killing has advanced. There are necessary and just wars. But that very fact says that we, as God's people, have not done all our duty. The calling of Christians, as set out clearly in Jesus' Sermon on the Mount, is to be peacemakers. Remember that peace is not simply the cessation or absence of fighting. Peace means a positive relationship of acceptance and love between and among people. Remember that the word *shalom*—peace—emphasizes wholeness, completeness, a lack of brokenness.

Talking about peace is very common, but actually practicing peace is much less common. Since 1948, and even before, our world has witnessed a continuing conflict between Jews and Palestinians for dominance in that troubled land where Micah lived long ago. Among both the Hebrew-speaking Jews and the Arabic-speaking Palestinians, the common greeting is "peace"—*shalom* in Hebrew; *salam* in Arabic. But there has been a notable lack of "doing peace." It is our duty as Christians to work for peace in the world.

How can we achieve peace? First our own hearts must be changed, and that can come about only through letting God work that miracle of change in our minds and hearts. We often use the word *conversion* in speaking of the change God can and will make in our lives. That word means *to change*. When the change is made inside us, the change also appears on the outside. God changes us from haters of others to lovers of others. When we are changed to those who love even our enemies—that is when we experience what peace really is.

Is peace really possible? Yes, indeed. People left to their own devices cannot achieve it. But with God, peace and all other good things are possible.

TEACHING PLANS

Teaching Plans—Varied Learning Activities

Connect with Life

1. Prepare a poster that has headlines/images cut from recent newspapers and magazines. Include headlines that speak of conflict in the world, fighting between nations or groups of people. Make sure to cover as much of the poster as possible, and leave room at the top of the poster for the words *When Will There Be Peace?* Place the poster on the board or somewhere it will be easily seen by the class.

2. Ask, *Is peace really an option in the world today?* Allow class members to respond. Then invite members to give their idea or definition of peace.

3. Have someone read aloud the Main Idea for the lesson: "God will provide peace to people who respond in faithfulness to him." State that the aim of this lesson is to create an awareness of God's peace and what it is and to bring a commitment to live a life that is faithful to God. Lead the class in prayer, asking God to give the strength necessary for this commitment.

Guide Bible Study

4. Note that Micah 4:1-4 is a definite change in tone from Micah 3:12. Ask, *What might be the purpose of having this passage of a "beginning" next to one that specifically tells of an "ending"?*

5. Have class members read 4:2-4 and look for the following elements:

   - Who is included in this prophecy
   - Who is not included (if applicable)
   - Why (if applicable) some people might be excluded
   - The contrast between God's house (4:2) and Jerusalem under the control of people (3:12)

   Give members an opportunity to report their findings.

6. Ask, *Is this vision of peace something that is seen to occur at some distant point in the future, or a possibility of things for the here and now?* Refer as needed to the discussion of the Hebrew understanding of prophecy found in the *Study Guide* under the heading, "Is Judgment God's Final Word?"

7. Read aloud verses 5-7, asking members to find the following:

   - The contrast between people placing their trust in false gods and placing their trust in Yahweh (4:5)
   - Who God calls to be his remnant (4:6)
   - The position of those who once were "driven away" (4:6-7)

   Ask, *Why are these people, the remnant, being treated with God's blessing?*

8. Have members read verses 8-13 to themselves and then comment on these questions:

   - What is the importance of verse 8? (Israel and Judah will one day be restored.)
   - Who is it that is being redeemed in verse 10?
   - Based on verses 11-13, who is eventually going to prevail?

9. Inquire, *Suppose you were alive at the time of these words. What emotions might you have felt at this point?* Encourage class members to respond.

10. Have someone read Micah 5:2-5 aloud. Have the class members find and tell where the following items are found in this passage:

    - Promise of ruler to come from the least of Judah's clans (5:2)
    - Time of arrival for this ruler (5:3)
    - Role of the ruler in the lives of the people (5:4a)

- The lifestyle of the people then compared to the lifestyle to come (5:4b)

  For help with responses, refer to "A Different Kind of Messiah" in the *Study Guide.*

11. Ask, *How will this ruler bring about the promises Micah makes?* (See the *Study Guide* under the heading, "The Fulfillment of Micah's Prophecy.")

Encourage Application

12. Ask, *What is the difference between trying to live in harmony with others and being a "doormat"?* Have someone read Matthew 5:9 aloud. Encourage members to respond in light of Christ's directive.

13. Read to class members the small article titled, "A Teachable Moment," in the *Study Guide.* After reading, divide the class into two groups, having each give biblical support as needed to their answers to the questions at the end of the article.

14. Use these questions to guide further discussion about peace, especially in the church: *What are some things that happen in our church that would cause conflict? How can an individual bring about peace? How can I help bring peace to any conflicts within our church?* Have class members write down on a piece of paper two things they can do that will help bring peace to conflicts within the church.

15. Close the lesson in prayer, asking God to bring God's peace into the lives of the class members, the church, and their families.

Teaching Plans—Lecture and Questions

Connect with Life

1. Inform class members that today's lesson continues Micah's proclamations of God's faithfulness. Read aloud the Main Idea for the lesson: "God will provide peace to people who respond in faithfulness to him."

2. Read the following quote from Thomas à Kempis, "First keep the peace within yourself, then you can also bring peace to others."[1] Ask class members to silently evaluate whether their lives would bring others peace.

3. Suggest that today's lesson will help us understand the peace God provides and commit ourselves to live for him. Lead the class in prayer, asking God to give illumination to the Scriptures and especially to God's desire for peace in our lives.

Guide Bible Study

4. Read Micah 4:1-5 aloud, drawing members' attention to the hopeful tone of the opening verses (compared to the closing verse of Micah 3). Explain, using the *Study Guide*, the Hebrew understanding of prophecy in the first paragraph under "Is Judgment God's Final Word?" Ask, *Is this prophecy inclusive or exclusive?* (inclusive; intended for people from "many nations") *What implications does this have?*

5. Read verses 6-8 aloud, having members look for the following things:

   - Who was being gathered (4:6)
   - The purpose of the gathering (4:7)
   - What Jerusalem would be like at this time (4:8)

6. Comment on the traits of those whom God chose to be his remnant: weak, lame, exiled, grieving. Ask, *Who might these people be?*

7. Read 5:2-5 aloud. Ask one or two members to summarize this passage in their own words. Then compare 4:1-4 with 5:2-5, explaining to the class the message of peace that is present in both.

8. Ask, *What was the purpose of the promised Ruler? How would this Ruler change the lives of the people?* Note that the rule of the Shepherd Ruler would not depend on military might, but on God's peace.

9. From the *Study Guide*, read aloud the small article titled "*Shalom.*" Then ask members to give examples of how the Shepherd Ruler of 5:4-5 would bring *shalom* to the people.

10. Read Matthew 5:9 aloud, and ask class members to give examples of *where* we are to be peacemakers.

Encourage Application

11. Ask, *What is the difference between living peacefully with others and being a "doormat"?* Encourage members to look at their own lives and consider how they practice living peacefully with others.

12. From the *Study Guide*, read aloud the small article titled "A Teachable Moment?" Use the questions at the end of the article to guide discussion.

13. Ask, *Is there presently a problem in the church in which you personally are involved? How can we become peacemakers within the church family?* Have class members write on a piece of paper two things they can do to bring peace within the church.

14. Close the lesson in prayer, asking God for guidance and thanking God for his peace.

NOTES

1. Justin Kaplan, ed., *Bartlett's Familiar Quotations*, 16th Edition (Boston, MA: Little, Brown, & Co., 1992), 132:17.

Background

Micah 6—7

Main Idea

In response to God's grace, we are to express our faithfulness to him by showing justice and kindness toward other people.

Question to Explore

What does God want from you?

Teaching Aim

To lead participants to evaluate how they are fulfilling God's requirements and respond to God by showing justice and kindness toward other people

MICAH

What the Lord Requires

Lesson Fourteen

God's Case Against His People

BIBLE COMMENTS

Understanding the Context

The words of Micah were delivered to a rebellious people living in a time of what they saw as peaceful prosperity. But this was nothing more than a very thin veneer covering a terribly corrupt people who had gone far from the God to whom they had pledged faithfulness in the days of the formation of the nation in the wilderness.

The passage before us is bracketed by the covenant Israel made with Yahweh in the wilderness. It begins with the Lord reminding them of what he did for them when they were slaves in Egypt (6:4). It concludes with a prayer that God will again shepherd them as he did when they escaped from Egypt (7:14) and that God also will remember the promises made to their ancestors (7:18–20). The story of that covenant is told in Exodus 19—24, but the heart of the making of the covenant is found in Exodus 19:3–8.

We know from other ancient literature that covenants were common in the ancient Near East. Covenants were sometimes made between individuals or groups of equal rank and power. But some were between unequals—such as a great king and local chieftain or group of chieftains. This covenant between God and Israel is of the latter type. Yahweh was the great power; Israel was the weak and needy nation. It was based on the power of Yahweh, demonstrated in the delivering of the people from their Egyptian slavery and leading them to the mountain of the Lord.

Each of the covenant makers assumed certain obligations. The obligations Israel undertook were to keep God's laws, obey and follow God's leadership, and serve as God's priests in the world. Remember from our previous study that priests had the duty, in addition to officiating at sacrifices, of teaching the truths about God and how to worship and serve him. The responsibilities God assumed—*if Israel carried out their obligations*—were to claim them as his holy or set-apart nation, and to give them the distinctive duty of serving as his priests in the world. From Exodus 34:10–11 as well as many other passages, we learn that the possession of the land of Canaan was a part of God's promises in this covenant.

Much of the story of the Old Testament centers on this covenant, how Israel would fail in their obligations, repent, and fail again. In Micah 6:3–5 through the prophet God pointed out his deliverance of the people over and over. Instead of obedience to God his people had kept the statutes of Omri and Ahab—both notably godless rulers. But God never gives up on his people. He is ever ready to pardon the repentant.

Interpreting the Scriptures

God's Case Against His People (6:1–5)

6:1. The "controversy" theme appears again in this passage. It was a courtroom scene in which God brought his charge against his covenant people, people who had not lived up to the obligations they took upon themselves in the covenant. It was a cosmic court in which the mountains, the hills, and the enduring foundations of the earth were called to witness the charges.

6:3–5. God began by asking why they had been so faithless. *What have I done to get such a response from you?* Then God recited some of the great things he had done to care for his people. First, God freed them from slavery in Egypt. This calls to mind the plagues he sent on Egypt (Exodus 5—12) to win the people's freedom, as well as their deliverance at the sea when hemmed in by Egyptian forces (Ex. 14). He gave them impressive leadership in those times—Moses, their great leader; Aaron, their priest; and Miriam, a prophetess who was the sister of Moses and Aaron.

The people were next called to remember the events centering on Balak and Balaam. (Numbers 22—24). Balak was the king of the Moabites at the time the Hebrews in the wilderness, traveling toward Israel from Sinai, were moving into the plains of Moab. Moab is the area east of the northern part of the Dead Sea. Fearful of the strength of the Hebrews, Balak hired a well-known soothsayer or diviner named Balaam, from the region of the Euphrates River, to put a hex or a curse on these Hebrews either to destroy or diminish their power. Balaam came and tried, but failed. Every time he opened his mouth to curse the Hebrews, a blessing came out instead.

The people also were called to remember the events transpiring from the time they were at Shittim until they came to Gilgal. The events at Shittim came immediately after the confrontation with Balaam. Here the Hebrews were seduced into worship of Baal of Peor with its "sacred" prostitutes (Numbers 25). Yet God forgave them and led them on, after the death of Moses, under Joshua. From here also the spies were sent to scout out the city of Jericho (Joshua 2:1). After they crossed the Jordan, coming into the land of Canaan proper, they first camped at Gilgal to prepare for the taking of Jericho (Josh. 4).

Micah 6:5 concludes with " . . . that you may know the saving acts of the LORD." This should be enough to remind them of God's wonderful and forgiving care for his covenant people.

How to Respond to God's Love and Care (6:6–8)

6:6–7. The introductory question simply asks, *How shall I come before such a mighty God?* This is followed by three questions probing possibilities. Each is a rhetorical question, and each demands a negative answer. *Are burnt offerings of choice calves what God wants?* This might cost a bit, but it could easily be done. If not this, step up the value of the offering. *What about thousands of rams and ten thousands of rivers of oil? What more valuable offering could one give? Human sacrifice? The fruit of my body for the sin of my soul?* Again the demanded answer is, *No*.

6:8. What then? God had been telling his people all along. God's instructions are all made plain in the law, and the prophets had been calling for them. All God wants is what is good. Remember that in the Old Testament "good" is that which conforms to God's wishes, or what God's will for people truly is. Included are three things: "do justice"; "love kindness"; "walk humbly with your God."

Do justice! Justice is that which is right. Its origin is with God himself, and it comes forth out of the very essence of who God is. He is a righteous God. Justice was disclosed in the law, and it was promoted by the prophets and wise men of ancient Israel. Justice is expressed in how one treats others, especially the poor and downtrodden. They have no clout and no one to stand up for them against the powerful of the world. Do what is right for them, as you likely would for your friends. The law was given to establish justice, but it had been manipulated to benefit those in powerful places. Do what is right for everyone regardless of the cost. Why? Simply because that is what the will of God is for human beings. Thus it is good. Justice was a primary theme of the prophecy of Amos, who was incensed by the treatment the poor received. Micah affirmed this as one of the qualities God desires all people to possess in their lives.

Love kindness! Love this! Be devoted to it. We use the word "love" so glibly that it becomes almost meaningless. We love our husbands, our wives, our children, our friends, our church, our God; we also love chocolate pie. Remember that the kind of love of which the Bible speaks is that which led God to send his Son into the world to face shameful treatment at the hands of human beings and finally a cruel death on the cross. Love requires serious concern for the object of our love, even self-denial, and total commitment to the one or what we love.

What is it Micah urges us to love? Kindness? Yes, and much more. In Hebrew the word is *hesed.* The meaning of this word has been the subject of many articles and even some books. It has been translated in a variety of ways in different English Bibles. A sampling of these includes *loving-kindness, mercy, constant love, loyalty, being kind to others.* Hosea used the same word in 6:6: "I desire steadfast love [*hesed*] and not sacrifice. . . ." This is a covenant word, and its meaning relates to the covenant agreement Israel made with God. There is probably not a single word in the English language with which to translate the word. It means faithfulness to the covenant vows the nation had made with their God. The prophet called the Hebrews to be absolutely committed to complete faithfulness to the covenant and all it contained.

Walk humbly with your God! Remember from the previous lesson that "walk" does not mean *take a stroll* but *live your life.* The third part of

Micah's call for a true and pure religion is this: *Live your life with humility before your God.* Humility is the opposite of pride. Pride is the essence of sin. Look back to Genesis 3 and you will see that the temptation there was self-exalting pride, a pride that said, *I want to be God myself so that I will not need to look up to anyone.* Was that not the temptation: "you will be like God" (Genesis 3:5)? Living your life humbly with God means that you recognize and honor God as God and both understand and maintain the proper relationship with God (see Isaiah 2:11–12 about the dangers of pride).

In Micah 6:8, the prophet summarized some of the primary teachings of the other prophets with whom he shared ministry to God's people. Micah's definition of true religion (6:8) is not surpassed by any other statement in the Old Testament. No clearer understanding of what God wants and expects from God's people will be found until the teachings of Jesus. But the people of Micah's day fell short of what God expected of them.

Jerusalem Is Doomed (6:9–16)

Even hesitant to utter the name of the wicked city, Micah listed some of its sins, identified as "treasures of wickedness in the house of the wicked" (6:10). Wealth had been gained by dishonesty and deceit. Jerusalem would be punished by hunger, desolation, and shame. This punishment would come because they had followed the paths of Omri and Ahab— godless kings a generation earlier in the Northern Kingdom of Israel who had led that nation down the pathway to destruction.

No Righteous People Left (7:1–7)

The leaders of the city were totally corrupt. Even family members were not to be trusted—they all had become enemies. The only hope was to wait for God's salvation.

The Only Hope Is God (7:8–17)

God would vindicate the faithful of the land. He would care for them as in the days of old when they escaped from Egypt. Then the oppressing nations would be shamed.

The Wonder of a Forgiving God (7:18–20)

Micah marvels at a God who will pardon, forgive, and show such compassion for his people. God can be counted on to keep his promises. As

God throws all their sins into the ocean depths, God will remember the blessings promised to their ancestors.

Focusing on the Meaning

God is the same in every generation. He can be trusted and will never change. God still condemns sin and sinners. God also remembers promises, and God pardons and blesses those who repent and call on him. "Who is a God like you?" Micah asked in wonder, *Who can and will redeem such evil ones* (7:18).

Throughout the Bible, God certainly condemns the unrepentant one, but God always holds out a merciful and forgiving hand to one who sincerely seeks him. What about our sins? Only God can deal with them. They burden us and lead us to despair. But God takes them and throws them into the depths of the sea.

What has God done for you? For the Hebrews he had with his mighty power delivered them from the hands of cruel slave masters in Egypt, giving them a new life in Canaan. The Hebrews owed God their love and loyalty. What has God done for you? He has given, or offers to give, freedom from the slave master of sin and a new life for all eternity with him in the heavenly places he has prepared. What do you owe him? Certainly no less than the Hebrews owed their Deliverer.

We cannot sacrifice our way to God. To put it in modern terms, we cannot give our way to God. Micah set forth the same truth the psalmist knew: "For you have no delight in sacrifice; if I were to give a burnt offering, you would not be pleased. The sacrifice acceptable to God is a broken spirit; a broken and contrite heart, O God, you will not despise" (Psalm 51:16–17).

Israel had failed in their promise to keep the covenant made with God at the foot of Mount Sinai. Micah called the nation to return to keeping those vows. We do not live under that Old Covenant, but under a New Covenant, established by Christ himself. It was promised by Jeremiah (Jeremiah 31:31–34). This covenant is written not on stone as were the Old Covenant laws. They are written on our hearts. This promise was fulfilled by Christ, and we have the Holy Spirit to continue to engrave his commandments on our hearts. Micah challenges each of us to walk, to live our lives, in obedient service to our Lord.

What God wants from his people has not changed:

1. Do justice—what is right as God defines it, just because it is right.

2. Love faithfulness to your commitment made to God.

3. Live your life, not in the prideful desires of your heart, but in humility and obedience to God.

TEACHING PLANS

Teaching Plans—Varied Learning Activities

Connect with Life

1. Write on the board: *Expectations.* As members arrive, ask them to think about some important expectations that have been made of them. When all members have arrived, begin by sharing your experience, and then ask them to do the same.

2. Ask, *Have you ever been expected to do something and then did not do it? How did that make you feel? How did it make the other person feel?* Explain that today we are going to discuss the expectations of God for his people, and see what our response to God's expectations should be.

3. Have someone read aloud the Main Idea for this lesson: "In response to God's grace, we are to express our faithfulness to him by showing justice and kindness toward other people." Lead the class in prayer, asking God to reveal to you God's plan for treating others as illustrated in Micah.

Guide Bible Study

4. Point out that once again, we find the image of a court case in the Scriptures. Read Micah 6:1-2 aloud, and ask members to determine the following:

   - Who is speaking against the people of Israel? (God)
   - Who is to be the jury for the proceeding? (the mountains and depths of the earth)

- What has precipitated this proceeding? (Israel's continued covenant disobedience)

5. Have the class form two groups. One group is to approach the assignment from God's perspective and the other from Israel's perspective. Have each group read Micah 6:1-5 and then discuss the following question from the perspective assigned:

  - What evidence, if any, is there to show that your group has broken the covenant?
  - What specific actions were taken by your group to ensure the success of the covenant?
  - What is the plea of your group? (guilty or not guilty)

6. From the *Study Guide* under "A Day in Court," give some background information on 6:4–5, specifically on Balak and Balaam. Make particular note of the safe passage given from Shittim to Gilgal. Encourage members to recount times in their lives when God has given safe passage through times of trial or persecution.

7. Ask, *What was the purpose of God's repeating the acts on his part of the covenant?* Explain that the word "know" (6:5) refers to the personal, intimate meaning of the knowledge of God's faithfulness.

8. Have someone read 6:6-7 aloud. Note that the beginning sacrifice is accessible by most people, but then the level increases to the level of the wealthy and ends with the unthinkable—a child sacrifice. Ask, *How might we rephrase these questions today? What are some of the ways people try to establish a relationship to God with their own efforts? Are these more effective than the ones mentioned here?*

9. Have two members read Psalm 24:3 and Psalm 15:1, asking the class to listen to these verses and compare them to Micah 6:6-7. Ask the following questions:

  - What differences do you see between the Micah passage and the Psalms passages?
  - Is it a fair assessment to say that Micah 6:6-7 is saying something like, *Ok, what's it going to take for me to get right with you, Lord? What's it going to cost me?*
  - Do you think God is more concerned with our hearts or our sacrifices?

10. Using the *Study Guide*, explain to the class the possible meaning of verse 8. Note that the answer is directed to all people. ("You" refers to everyone. My English teacher used to say, "*You* applies to every man, woman, cat, and dog within the sound of your voice." Suffice it to say, if you are reading the passage, then "you" means *you!*)

11. Divide the class into three small groups, assigning them each a portion of verse 8: "do justice," "love kindness," "walk humbly with your God." Have each group define and illustrate what their phrase means to them and report back to the class after three or four minutes.

Encourage Application

12. Guide further discussion using these questions:

    - *What are some specific ways to practice justice?* Allow members a few moments for responses; then ask, *How can one express a commitment to kindness?*
    - *Are there any indications in the life of the church today that there is a rupture in our relationship with God? What are they?*
    - *What are some characteristics of an attentive walk with the Lord?* As members respond, write their responses on the board. Then ask, *How many of these characteristics do you possess?*

13. Close in prayer, asking God to show ways that class members can act this week in ways that are expressive of gratitude for God's grace.

Teaching Plans—Lecture and Questions

Connect with Life

1. To begin the lesson, ask, *What indications do you see that humility is a characteristic needed by God's people today?*

2. Share with the class the Main Idea for this week's lesson: "In response to God's grace, we are to express out faithfulness to him by showing justice and kindness towards other people."

3. Lead the class in prayer, asking for the Holy Spirit to bring a spirit of humility, justice, and kindness to all gathered together.

Guide Bible Study

4. Read aloud Micah 6:1-2, explaining to members who the active participants are in this court scene:

   - God (He brings the charge against the people.)
   - The mountains and the depths (They act as the jury.)
   - The people of Israel (They have broken the covenant with God.)

5. Read aloud verses 3-5 and ask the following questions:

   - How does God feel about the disobedience of the people?
   - How has God been active in their lives since their deliverance from Egypt?
   - What does this have to say for us today?

6. Using the *Study Guide*, explain the importance of Moses, Aaron, and Miriam to the covenant history of Israel. Explain further the other examples in 6:5–6 of God's actions through Israelite history, showing God's faithfulness and grace towards them.

7. Ask, *What is the importance of knowing God's acts? Why should we today be concerned with what God did more than 2,000 years ago?* List responses on the board.

8. Read Micah 6:6-7 aloud and use comments from the *Study Guide* about sacrifice to explain what matters most to God. Ask, *What are some ways that people today have tried to establish a relationship with God through their own efforts? Are these ways effective or ineffective?*

9. Have someone read aloud Micah 6:8. Ask, *Does this verse refer more to a giving of things or a giving of self?* Lead the class to evaluate their lives for a moment and see whether there are areas in which they could make improvements in their daily walk with God.

10. Use the *Study Guide* to explain the phrases in verse 8—"do justice," "love mercy," and "walk humbly with your God." Ask, *How might the general population respond to this? Would they feel they are accomplishing this?*

Encourage Application

11. State that as believers we need to demonstrate God's presence in our lives by how we interact and react to the world around us. Ask the following questions:

    • What are some specific ways to practice justice?
    • How can one express a commitment to kindness?
    • What are some characteristics of an attentive walk with God?

12. Ask, *Are there any indications that our relationship with God is broken today? If so, what are they?* Have class members write on a piece of paper things in people's lives that are hindering their relationship with God. Close in prayer by asking God to give discernment to class members so that they can live lives that will glorify God.

How to Order More Bible Study Materials

It's easy! Just fill in the following information. (Note: when the *Teaching Guide* is priced at $2.45, the *Teaching Guide* includes Bible comments for teachers.)

✤ = Texas specific

Title of item	Price	Quantity	Cost
This Issue:			
Amos, Hosea, Micah—Study Guide	$1.95	_____	_____
Amos, Hosea, Micah—Large Print Study Guide	$1.95	_____	_____
Amos, Hosea, Micah—Teaching Guide	$2.45	_____	_____
Previous Issues Available:			
God's Message in the Old Testament—Study Guide✤	$1.95	_____	_____
God's Message in the Old Testament—Teaching Guide✤	$1.95	_____	_____
Genesis 12—50: Family Matters—Study Guide	$1.95	_____	_____
Genesis 12—50: Family Matters—Large Print Study Guide	$1.95	_____	_____
Genesis 12—50: Family Matters—Teaching Guide	$2.45	_____	_____
Good News in the New Testament—Study Guide✤	$1.95	_____	_____
Good News in the New Testament—Large Print Study Guide✤	$1.95	_____	_____
Good News in the New Testament—Teaching Guide✤	$2.45	_____	_____
Isaiah and Jeremiah—Study Guide	$1.95	_____	_____
Isaiah and Jeremiah—Large Print Study Guide	$1.95	_____	_____
Isaiah and Jeremiah—Teaching Guide	$2.45	_____	_____
Matthew: Jesus As the Fulfillment of God's Promises— Study Guide✤	$1.95	_____	_____
Matthew: Jesus As the Fulfillment of God's Promises— Large Print Study Guide✤	$1.95	_____	_____
Matthew: Jesus As the Fulfillment of God's Promises— Teaching Guide✤	$2.45	_____	_____
Jesus in the Gospel of Mark—Study Guide	$1.95	_____	_____
Jesus in the Gospel of Mark—Large Print Study Guide	$1.95	_____	_____
Jesus in the Gospel of Mark—Teaching Guide	$2.45	_____	_____
Gospel of John—Study Guide	$1.95	_____	_____
Gospel of John—Large Print Study Guide	$1.95	_____	_____
Gospel of John—Teaching Guide	$2.45	_____	_____
Acts: Sharing God's Good News with Everyone—Study Guide✤	$1.95	_____	_____
Acts: Sharing God's Good News with Everyone — Teaching Guide✤	$1.95	_____	_____
Romans: Good News for a Troubled World—Study Guide✤	$1.95	_____	_____
Romans: Good News for a Troubled World—Teaching Guide✤	$1.95	_____	_____
1 Corinthians—Study Guide	$1.95	_____	_____
1 Corinthians—Large Print Study Guide	$1.95	_____	_____
1 Corinthians—Teaching Guide	$2.45	_____	_____
Galatians: By Grace Through Faith, and Ephesians: God's Plan and Our Response—Study Guide✤	$1.95	_____	_____
Galatians: By Grace Through Faith, and Ephesians: God's Plan and Our Response—Large Print Study Guide✤	$1.95	_____	_____
Galatians: By Grace Through Faith, and Ephesians: God's Plan and Our Response—Teaching Guide✤	$2.45	_____	_____
Hebrews and James—Study Guide	$1.95	_____	_____
Hebrews and James—Large Print Study Guide	$1.95	_____	_____
Hebrews and James—Teaching Guide	$2.45	_____	_____
Coming for use beginning September 2003			
Philippians, Colossians, Thessalonians—Study Guide	$1.95	_____	_____
Philippians, Colossians, Thessalonians—Large Print Study Guide	$1.95	_____	_____
Philippians, Colossians, Thessalonians—Teaching Guide	$2.45	_____	_____

Beliefs Important to Baptists

Who in the World Are Baptists, Anyway? (one lesson)	$ .45	_____	_____
Who in the World Are Baptists, Anyway?—Teacher's Edition	$ .55	_____	_____
Beliefs Important to Baptists: I (four lessons)	$1.35	_____	_____
Beliefs Important to Baptists: I—Teacher's Edition	$1.75	_____	_____
Beliefs Important to Baptists: II (four lessons)	$1.35	_____	_____
Beliefs Important to Baptists: II—Teacher's Edition	$1.75	_____	_____
Beliefs Important to Baptists: III (four lessons)	$1.35	_____	_____
Beliefs Important to Baptists: III—Teacher's Edition	$1.75	_____	_____
Beliefs Important to Baptists—Study Guide (one-volume edition; includes all lessons)	$2.35	_____	_____
Beliefs Important to Baptists—Teaching Guide (one-volume edition; includes all lessons)	$1.95	_____	_____

*Charges for standard shipping service:

Subtotal up to $20.00 $3.95
Subtotal $20.01—$50.00 $4.95
Subtotal $50.01—$100.00   10% of subtotal
Subtotal $100.01 and up   8% of subtotal

Please allow three weeks for standard delivery. For express shipping service: Call 1-866-249-1799 for information on additional charges.

Subtotal   _____

Shipping*   _____

TOTAL   _____

Number of FREE copies of *Brief Basics for Texas Baptists* needed for leading adult Sunday School department periods _____

_____

Your name   Phone

_____

Your church

_____

Mailing address

_____

City   State   Zip code

MAIL this form with your check for the total amount to
BAPTISTWAY PRESS
Baptist General Convention of Texas
333 North Washington
Dallas, TX 75246-1798
(Make checks to "Baptist Executive Board.")

OR, **FAX** your order anytime to: 214-828-5187, and we will bill you.

OR, **CALL** your order toll-free: 1-866-249-1799 (8:30 a.m.-5:00 p.m., M-F), and we will bill you.

OR, **E-MAIL** your order to our internet e-mail address: baptistway@bgct.org, and we will bill you.

We look forward to receiving your order! Thank you!